Wine or curry

A language te_____ _ ____,

Foreword

Some say that life can change drastically in a week, let alone within the space of four years, which is roughly the same period of time as Britain has been leaving the European Union - but the less said about that debacle, the better.

From silent and efficient public transport, to elaborately decorated musical buses.

From supermarkets equipped with highly irritating self-service machines, to supermarkets which would be more fitting in a post-apocalyptic era.

From a school with knife detectors on entry, to a school with security guards so friendly that any impostors would be welcomed like Prince William and Kate on a world tour.

From a body building macho husband, to a Zen Buddhist rock star life partner.

Not forgetting the best, the bizarre, and now irreversible change from wine to curry for breakfast.

Contents

Chapter one: Up to my eyeballs in Panaculty

Monday, 24th November 2014

Chester, England

"Go on. This might be the only time you ever wear a mortarboard. Do the standard pose, and throw it into the air!" said mum, grinning. After finishing our studies in May we were finally celebrating our graduation a few months later. I had already begun my teacher training in York, and had taken a day off in order to attend my graduation. Most graduation ceremonies usually happen in July or August, but our university had to wait until the back end of November for a slot at the beautiful Chester cathedral. I never realised before that Cathedrals could actually be so busy; they are graceful and elegant buildings that are an integral part of every British city, but I always believed that their main purpose of existing was for tourists, school trips, carol services at Christmas and the odd wedding. But I had been wrong. Cathedrals clearly had a much more fulfilling social life than me.

I looked across at my friend Ffion and on the count of three; we lobbed our mortarboard hats into the air with as much force and enthusiasm as we could muster. Well, Ffion threw hers much more graciously and in the picture perfect way that one often sees on university prospectuses. As mum eagerly tried to snap some memorable photographs and videos, which was already a great feat owing to her lack of technological

3

confidence, I dived to capture mine as it fell, fearing bad luck for eternity if I did not grasp the wretched thing. I grabbed the hat, but in my panic I stumbled and fell flat on my face in front of everybody. At this point I'm not sure how the whole bad luck theory worked, but what I did know was that it was the only snap that my mum had managed to take. Maybe it was just a sign of what was to come; that I would fall down, but brush it all off, and get back up again.

Almost a year later

Monday, 19th October 2015
Gateshead, Tyne and Wear, England

The alarm blared, offending my ears at this ungodly hour, and I woke with a start, flailing my arms around feebly in a half desperate, half zombie like attempt to reach my phone to silence this unwelcome din.

The winter nights were beginning to set in, and at this time of year the sun wouldn't even rise until around nine in the morning, and would set between four and five in the afternoon. This contributed to the fact that the first term in the academic year was always particularly brutal. My daily commute to and from school were for the most part cloaked in what seemed like eternal darkness. I do suppose that Gateshead could have been an ideal choice of location for Steven Spielberg if he ever wanted to produce a vampire movie. In addition to the everlasting darkness, the persistent damp and drizzle and the drab concrete pavement slabs set the scene perfectly, framing the streets like horizontal gravestones.

I clocked the time. 6.18 am. There was just two more precious minutes of comfort before I reluctantly had to face the day. As always, those two minutes passed in what felt like a nanosecond, and with my limbs feeling like the weight of a week's worth of food shopping, I hauled myself out of bed. It was no secret that I certainly was not a morning person at all; or a self-confessed *'Morgenmuffel'* as one says in German.

Before the era of mobile phones, I used to have an alarm clock with wheels which would manoeuver itself assertively around the room until I would drag myself out of my cesspit with an elevated blood pressure and a highly unreasonable disdain for something which was just doing its job. Needless to say, it didn't last long before it was thrown out of the window. I always wondered what it must be like to belong to the *other side*, the side of 'morning people'. My mum used to say that it's something to do with the time you were born. Those who were born early in the morning will be morning larks. Those who were born late at night will be night owls. I was born in the evening and my brother in the morning, and we both perfectly fit our mum's theory. I'm not sure how this theory works for anyone born on the cusp, at midday or midnight, so hopefully someone who is stuck for an idea for their research thesis can steal this one and we will all find out in a few years.

The kitchen of 3 Grove Terrace really looked like my life was much more fun than it actually was. Empty wine bottles littered the worktops, decorated with the occasional ready meal packet or egg box, which our cat, Zizou Wazizi, often took great pleasure at sitting her sleek furry backside in. I hurriedly made myself a strong coffee, the first of several I would undoubtedly consume during a typical school day. Finding nothing in the fridge to eat – not that there would be time even for a quick bowl of Muesli anyway, I grabbed the essentials; phone, keys, purse and bag - and strode boldly out of the door to the Nissan Juke parked outside.

Note how I mention 'the' Nissan Juke, not 'my' Nissan Juke. My partner Daniel worked at the Nissan factory on the outskirts of Sunderland seven miles away, and one of the benefits of the job was a lucrative company car scheme. When my friends from other parts of the country came to visit, they always remarked that they had never seen so many Nissan Juke's and Qashquai's in one place, which was probably true, as the Nissan factory was without a doubt the largest employer in the north east of England. The money was good, but from what I understood, the job was exhausting, mind-numbing, and repetitive. Daniel always complained that it challenged his body and not his mind.

Daniel and I had only been seeing each other for about a year before deciding to move in together, and had opted to rent 3 Grove Terrace on the basis that it was within a reasonable distance for both of us to travel to work, as work does unfortunately seem to make up ninety percent of your life, like it or not. It wasn't bad at all for a first place, if you consider the fact that it was my first house *post* five years of student accommodation. If you have ever been brave enough to set foot inside an average student house, I'm sure you'll understand what I mean here. If not, then I'll enlighten you slightly. In my final year of university, the landlord had paid much more attention to lecturing us on at least three occasions about the four different types of fire extinguisher that we should use in case of a fire, than to the fact that he had charged us an astronomical cleaning fee and not cleaned the place at all. He had without a doubt used the payments from all six of us to go off on holiday with his wife, who was clearly only with him for the extortionate amount of money he made from exploiting students.

When we had moved into the dingy abyss, it was clear that the landlord had indeed pocketed the money, or had employed a cleaner with an extreme reversal of OCD. The dust on the curtains and worktops must have been at least two centimetres thick, dead flies and spiders littered every windowsill, and the cupboard doors were hanging off in such a state that it was quite probable someone had set off a firework in there as a joke. When my friend Bella and her parents had challenged the landlord about this, he said that he couldn't see a problem. Bella's dad had replied with his wonderful Yorkshire charm.

"Can't see a problem!? Even David Blunkett could bloody see this!"

(I'm not sure if I can get into trouble here for name dropping a famous politician, but it's not like he can see anyway, so hopefully I'm safe).

The landlord was furious at such conflict, and a few days later we found the internet router submerged in a bucket of water. Unfortunately we had no proof of course, but it was certainly him.

I hadn't always wanted to be a teacher, and when I gained qualified teacher status in 2014, it came as a real shock to all who had known me during my unruly teenage days. I had despised any form of authority from Year 8 onwards, and had certainly never hidden the fact. Amazingly, I had sailed through my GCSE's having barely revised, and had very quickly realized that A levels would not be the same at all. I had gone to a university that had previously been a teaching college, and had gained university status in 2005. There is often a lot of pressure from parents and society in general to go to a 'Russell group' university where the real hoity toity's go, and have been going for generations. I felt that I wouldn't fit in somewhere that was very prestigious and instead chose where I wanted to study based on the course combination I wanted to do. The main worry that my mum had was that I would end up at a university which is often referred to by the older generation as 'the old polytechnic'. I never was quite sure what she actually meant.

Although I hoped that I had made the right choice, the University of Chester unfortunately attracted many students from upper class backgrounds who had fallen short of mummy and daddy's expectations of Cambridge, Oxford, or Bristol, and although they were going to a university which was a bit further down the Times list, Chester was still a respectable enough place to live, so it was ok. My first year as a fresher had not been fun, and had really not lived up to my expectations of what university life would be like.

My grandma had been thrilled of course, and in the months leading up to my departure to begin my studies in Chester she had filled me with her chirpy reassurances at every opportunity:

"The first one in the family to go to uni like! Eeee, me bairn!"
"Eeeeeee, we'll all miss you here hinny, but you'll all be in the same boat, pet!"

My grandparents and mum were Geordies, and my granddad especially was fiercely proud of being so, along with his Scottish heritage, and he would happily divulge our family history to anyone who would care to listen. My grandma was always trying to feed everyone, and make everyone feel better about whatever crisis or problem they were facing, even if they were complete strangers. Warmth and friendliness towards strangers are qualities that Geordies are generally known for, as well as the unique dialect: the use of words such as canny, hinny, scran, bairn, radgie and gadgie to name a few. Geordies are also known for the creation of the bakery chain Greggs, which opened its first store in Gosforth and began to really take off while I was studying my A levels at Newcastle College. Greggs sell large plate sized buns known as *stotties,* which can contain a full Sunday dinner or full English breakfast inside. They were traditionally invented as a practical and filling meal for the miners to take down the shafts, and have been enjoying a revival as everyone who visits Newcastle runs into Greggs to sample one of the famous *stotties.*

Once I moved to Chester, I was bright eyed, bushy tailed and had many hopes for a new start. As soon as I arrived, I did what any normal person in the north east would do, and went straight to the pub across the road. In Newcastle, or in fact in any train station or airport pub, I would usually get chatting to someone within minutes; however here was a different ball game. I found that my first impression of people in Chester was that they were colder and more reserved than in the north east, and there seemed to be a real 'if you're not a somebody, I don't want to know you' sort of culture.

In some aspects it was actually quite fortunate that it took me so long to form a social circle, and I had persevered and focused heavily on my studies, something that I had definitely not done during my time 'studying' for my A levels at Newcastle College. Having a bar on campus and several more just a stone's throw away, combined with extremely friendly and vibrant people, meant that avoiding distractions (often in the form of casual drinks that rapidly turned into parties) was almost impossible.

By my second year at university thankfully, I had made a close knit group of like-minded friends, with whom I am still to this day very close. I graduated in 2013 with an upper second class combined degree in Modern Foreign Languages & International Development, and then went on to complete my PGCE (teacher training) in York the subsequent year, in which I had flourished. I recall as I threw that mortarboard cap into the air on graduation day how bright and promising the future had looked, and for once my poor mother was able to have something to be proud of instead of constant chaos she had dealt with during my turbulent teenage years.

On this dreary Monday morning however, as I squinted through the clouded windscreen, the wipers swinging urgently at full pelt as I battled my way through the atrocious weather, I pulled into the school car park, the feeling of a 'bright and promising future' was well and truly thousands of miles away. I had been offered a post at the school in Doncaster where I had completed my final teacher training placement and which I had really loved. Daniel unfortunately didn't want to leave the north east, and very fairly mentioned that he had come down to York almost every weekend while I was completing my training and if we were to continue this on a more permanent basis the relationship was probably not going to work. I had therefore applied for the first job of the season that I had seen advertised on the Times education website and desperately rushed to accept the post once it was offered following the interview, without first properly researching the school. This was a terrible decision which I would learn to thoroughly regret.

From the outside, Panaculty Academy was an impressive sight, its purple and grey façades smart with their first ever coat of paint, its automatic doors gliding smoothly open and closed without the faintest squeak. The appearance of the school was a huge disillusion to the pandemonium that lurked within. Once through those gleaming double doors designed to lure Her Majesty's Ofsted inspectors into a false pretence, you were practically in a detention centre, or maybe even a zoo. On high insight, I should have paid more attention to the airport style metal detectors which were situated just behind the main entrance, and realised that they had been installed for a very serious reason. It clearly was not just sweeties that were being confiscated here. I later discovered that although the school was brand spanking new, looks certainly were deceiving, especially as it had been created so that the council could save money by closing down two schools on opposite sides of the town, meaning that two previously warring communities had now been forced together.

I locked the car, grabbed my trolley with the books that I had spent the previous evening marking, and ran inside to get out of the relentless rain.

After opening my classroom door, the chemical smell of brand new carpet and furniture seeped in through every pore. I fired up the computer, bringing up my register for my Year 9 tutor group who would soon arrive, a 'word wheel' literacy starter that would hopefully wake them all up on this bleary Monday morning, and my PowerPoint on introducing the future tense in French for my first class of the day: Year 8 set 3. I had stayed up until the early hours of the morning perfecting this PowerPoint, which was complete with an engaging 'Mystic Meg predicting your future in French' YouTube video which I had made the night before. The students did not love French, but they did love YouTube. At Panaculty Academy, the head of department did not believe in textbooks, and so every single resource had to be made from scratch. As a newly qualified teacher, this added workload was extremely difficult to manage, though I had never said anything in fear of appearing weak or not good enough.

After the 15 minute form period and a very hurried dash to the photocopier, I had a quick glance over the presentation, making sure that the background colour was 'duck egg blue' instead of white, which was proven to help children who were dyslexic, I arrived back at my classroom to see that some of Year 8 Set 3 were already there waiting. Trying to stomp out the feeling of dread which was already pooling in the pit of my stomach, I raced to think of something positive about them – *anything*... well, at least they'd actually come to the lesson. Students at Panaculty Academy were often caught bunking off, and swiftly escorted back to their lessons by the senior management team, which was all they seemed to do despite their enormous salaries. When they were not wandering the corridors, they could often be found huddled together in their office over a box of doughnuts, deciding which teacher (usually the young and inexperienced ones) they would bully next.

Unlocking the door, I let the first wave of insults and complaints of the day wash over me. I was so prepared for them all now. The best coping mechanism was to stop caring, which it had sadly taken too long for me to realise. I had been determined to help students from the most disadvantaged backgrounds to make something of their lives as I had done, however as my mum Jennifer had said over and over again, "you can't help those who don't want to be helped."

"Why do we have to do French, miss? I speak *English*. I live in *England,* not France. I'm only ever going to learn English."

"My mam says this is a load of shite, miss."

"French people all speak English anyway, like *everyone* in the whole world speaks English!"

"Why did you ring my mum on Friday afternoon and grass on me, miss? She says she's gonna knock you right out for waking the baby up like!"

"I hate French me like."

If it had been just one or two students who were a pain, it would have been perfectly manageable. I had been praised for my classroom management during my training. However here it was the entire class, and every lesson was like fighting a losing battle.

"So much happiness on a Monday morning, eh?" I forced a fake and overly cheery smile, and bounced my voice up several octaves in a bid to stop the already rapidly souring atmosphere from declining any further. Ignoring me, the Year 8 pupils thundered into the classroom, already squawking about Ashlynn's selfies on Instagram, and who Cody-Lee's new girlfriend was. They shoved their French books that I had carefully and painstakingly spent marking until midnight the night before onto the floor and leaned back in their chairs exaggeratedly chewing gum, either glaring at me with an unsettlingly defiant look on their faces, or exchanging whispers behind cupped hands. Although I was used to this and had been warned during my teacher training that 'they will hate you just because you are there', certain classes often made me feel extremely uncomfortable.

Before I could even say "bonjour, comment allez-vous?" Django, one of the many traveller children in my class, ever so kindly blurted out:

"Miss, there's a pube on your neck."

The class erupted into fits of laughter, and I knew with a sinking feeling that there was no way that this day was going to be any different than any other that I had experienced so far at Panaculty Academy. I had entered the profession keen and eager to motivate and inspire those from 'hard to reach backgrounds', and was keen to work with traveller children. However, having at least five or six of them in a class of sometimes over thirty made that task absolutely impossible – a word which I had refused to believe in until recently.

The seating plans for each of my classes were heavily annotated to account for each student who had a special educational need, for those having a behavioural, emotional, or social difficulty, or for those who were from low income backgrounds and were entitled to free school meals. The appearance of a blank space on a seating plan here was a total rarity. The 'free school meals (FSM)' children, or 'pupil premium (PP)' children as they were later referred to as, were a particular area of focus for the school as the UK government had finally acknowledged that there was a huge attainment gap between students from the upper and middle classes and those from working class backgrounds.

Although it was great that the government wanted to address this issue, they went about it entirely the wrong way. They wanted each school to be able to provide extra information about each 'FSM' or 'PP' student and to be able to show data that they were making good progress. What they didn't realise and should have understood, was that all of the additional time that was taken up in order to obsess over data and progress took away the essential one to one time where teachers could nurture these students and give them the help that they may not be able to access at home.

Twenty minutes later into the lesson it was already five minutes past nine, and it was due to end at nine forty. Each lesson at Panaculty Academy lasted 55 minutes, but the amount of learning that took place during each of these lessons was very questionable. It had taken me over twenty minutes to calm the class down, having to send out three students: two for disregarding their first and second warnings for disruptive behaviour, and Django, who was being persistently insolent. Time had also been taken up having to find alternative classrooms for the students who had been sent out of my lesson, but then other teachers who also couldn't have them in their classrooms would send them back where they had come from. It was utterly hopeless.

"So you just basically add 'ai' onto the end to make it in the future tense then? Like *je joue au badminton* will become *je jouerai au badminton?*"

Like an oasis in the middle of an arid desert, I saw a glimmer of hope and relief. Maybe the self-made 'Mystic Meg predicts your future' YouTube video that I had made in a desperate bid to capture their attention the night before had actually made a slight difference.

"Oui, bien sûr!" I beamed widely at Kacey McCahill, a girl with a hard face and a loud mouth, but I could tell that deep down she wanted to do something more positive with her life. Kacey had a twin brother called Kevin, however they lived separately. One lived with their mother who was a raging alcoholic, and the other with the father, who seemingly brought back a different woman from the pub every other night. Social workers were in and out of the school on a daily basis, and I knew for sure that some of the many students that were discussed in the meetings were the McCahill's.

Over sixty per cent of the students in this school were free school meal (FSM) kids, which meant that their household income was deemed so low that the government would provide breakfast and lunch for them at school, and statistically they are much less likely than their classmates from more affluent backgrounds to achieve 5 good GCSE's. I saw many of these students arrive at school in the morning dishevelled, unwashed, and hungry. Thankfully unlike the management, the kitchen staff were a solid cornerstone of the school. They were a wonderful bunch of women who took great pride in their work, and cooked up wholesome breakfasts and lunches without fail every day.

The students were beginning to write a short paragraph predicting the future of their classmate using the verbs that they had identified in the YouTube video and for five minutes, it appeared that progress was actually happening. I smiled to myself for the first time in a long time. Evidence of written work in books would surely please the management and get them off my back for a little while. Although strategies for getting the students to speak spontaneously had been my strength in my training year, I had been forbidden to do anything other than grammar and writing as it was very difficult to record the evidence. As the Ofsted inspectors wouldn't be able to see it, speaking was deemed a pointless activity by the senior members of the department. As if I was actually Mystic Meg predicting the future, the two most volatile members of senior management, Jessica Renfrew and Debbie Ross, slunk into the back of the classroom, their pens poised like weaponry ready to fire above their jotters, their beady eyes ready to find any strand of hair out of place.

I was so relieved that they had chosen to grace my classroom with their presence now and not half an hour earlier. Apart from having to confiscate the odd fidget spinner and mobile phone the lesson ended much better than expected, and although these Year 8 students had a heck of a long way to go before the majority would get anywhere near their targets, they had done something! The lesson ended promptly and instead of the usual mad stampede out of the door, a couple of students even stayed behind to finish their written work. *Hallelujah!!!*

Unfortunately, Jessica and Debbie didn't recognise any of these minor successes.

"They haven't responded in red pen!" spat Jessica, her cheeks blotchy, thrusting Brandon McRae's open book at me in an uncontrollable rage.

"They haven't done their corrections. Their dates and titled aren't underlined as clearly stipulated in the 'beautiful books' section of our whole school marking policy. Which you, as a teacher in this school, are obliged to follow. Is this just a game to you?" roared her colleague and fellow staff slayer, Debbie.

I refused to look at either of them and bit my lip carefully. I really couldn't handle being yelled at, and I wanted to yell back at them that children like Brandon McRae had more pressing issues than making sure their date and title was underlined, and that they should have seen that even Kacey McCahill had miraculously shown enough interest to ask a question about French. All they cared about were a small team of Ofsted inspectors. In a desperate attempt to lighten my rapidly declining mood, I pictured the members of senior management lying naked on top of stacks of exercise books, legs akimbo, waving green and red pens and brandishing dildos with 'Ofsted' etched on them in diamante bling.

"I always give them 5 minutes of DIRT (dedicated improvement and reflection time) at the beginning of the lesson. But they just sit chatting and they won't do it," I said flatly.
"I can't physically force them to do it, and if I were to give them a break time detention they either wouldn't turn up, or the parents would complain that they had a detention for not underlining their dates and titles." I was careful to pronounce each syllable, as if speaking to an infant who wanted a chocolate ice cream, but I had to explain that there was only vanilla.

Sadly, this approach had the undesired effect of angering the vultures further.

"Won't do it? They won't do it? So now you're blaming the students for your incompetence? Are you for real? Wake up and take responsibility for the fact that THIS – IS - NOT – GOOD – ENOUGH! What will Ofsted say when they come? Where is the evidence of progress in these books? WHERE???"

I really wanted to say, "you don't understand a word of French, *that's* why you can't see the progress..." but I really didn't want to indulge in a shower of spit in yet another of their unnecessary meltdowns.

"You know… some people just aren't cut out to be a teacher. Maybe you should think about doing something else. You're not a natural. You just haven't got the knack for it. Why don't you go and observe one of Suzanne Powell's lessons? She literally has the students eating out of her hand. Maybe she could teach you what you should have learned in your training year. Trainees aren't what they used to be, don't you think Debbie? The standard is declining drastically."
They swooped off down the corridor, undoubtedly to go and 'type up their findings' of my lesson with much exaggeration so I could be called in for a bollocking by the head or the deputy if he couldn't be bothered.

Teaching used to be the same as nursing when it came to pay, and you would move up the pay scale with each year of experience. However, the government decided to bring in something called 'performance related pay.' This was fantastic for the more senior members of staff and terrible for anyone ranking below head of department – basically, any teacher. I was sure that senior management had a monopoly on which classes they wanted, so they could always meet the targets that were set at the beginning of the year and they could easily get their bonus. The young and inexperienced teachers like me got all of the really difficult classes so that we could be kept on the lowest pay scale, and more bonuses could go into the pockets of the senior management, and they could get that nice Audi they wanted.

The attack from senior management had eaten up most of my free period designated for planning lessons and marking books, and now I was jittery with panic as the time I had planned to use to get ready for the following lesson had now disappeared into thin air. As a newly qualified teacher I was required to teach twenty seven lessons per week, and entitled to three free periods per week, which was nowhere near enough time to get anything done. I would often end up taking two boxes of books home with me to do my marking, which was by far the most laborious and tedious aspect of teaching. Also, it was pretty soul destroying when the students would rarely even take any notice of the endless comments that a teacher in this academy was obliged to write. We had to include a comment about what went well, a comment about how to improve, and also create a question targeted specifically to each student, to which there had to be evidence of a student response in red pen. Teachers at Panaculty Academy also had to mark in green, as red was deemed to be too aggressive.

Looking at the clock and shaking, I hurriedly recorded the positive and negative marks on SIMS, the computer software which is used by most schools in England. I had seven minutes, of which five were easily taken up by recording Kacey McCahill's positive mark, and writing explanations for why three children had had to be removed from the classroom. With two minutes remaining I dashed to the photocopier and quickly bashed the buttons in an attempt to make it copy the river diagrams for my following lesson faster. The next lesson was Year 9 Geography. As I had an A level in Geography, I was asked to teach it alongside French and German so that the school didn't have to spend money hiring another teacher. The photocopier wailed a loud and whingey 'beeeeeeep', and I prepared myself for the worst, but unfortunately the expected.

Credit balance: 00.03. Insufficient funds. Noooooooo!

In an effort to reduce paper wastage, and more importantly in the eyes of management, to save money, the school policy was that teachers were granted photocopying credit of five pounds per term. Once that expired they had to top up from their own pockets. Now, given that a term usually lasts between three and four months, and that I taught 27 lessons per week, with an average of 30 students per class, and that there were no textbooks in my department because either, the head of department didn't believe in textbooks, or didn't want to spend any of the budget on them, five pounds of photocopying credit was nowhere near enough. This time I had managed to make it stretch until the fifth week of term before running out.

Just at the right moment, I spied Louise Haughty, the head of French, ambling down the corridor. Although mid-fifties and quite cuddly and warm looking, her bitter and cold personality did not at all reflect her appearance. I was sure that I had never once seen her smile in the whole year I had worked here. I suspected that she too was under a lot of pressure from the senior management, though it certainly wasn't an excuse to take it out on other members of staff.

"Louise, do you have any photocopy credit I could possibly borrow?" I pleaded. Only one minute more to go and the bell would ring.

"You can't have run out already. What are you going to do for the rest of the term?" There was no concern in her voice, but a patronising edge to it.

"I don't know – find someone to hack the system maybe? Can you photocopy these sheets for me or not?" I knew I sounded slightly rude, but I really didn't have time to deal with this obscure woman. Louise Haughty tutted, a noise which grated on me as much as people who ate with their mouth open, and began to photocopy the river diagrams just as the bell rang. Success! At least I thought so for a moment. Louise stopped suddenly, and turned to face me.

"Hang on – this is Geography isn't it, not French?"

"Louise, come on man – the Geography department is two floors above, I don't have time to go running around up there. You have to agree that it doesn't make sense that I'm not given more photocopying credit, as I'm spread across Modern Languages and Geography?"

"That's something for you to take up with the management. It's not my duty to photocopy Geography for you! You can't expect the same treatment as you had in your training year, people holding your hand and giving you special help. You have to learn to manage your time and resources better."

I quickly grabbed the river diagrams and marched off at full speed towards my classroom so I could escape fast. I also needed to get there quickly before the Year 9's could do any considerable damage, and I definitely didn't have time to listen to the patronising princess and her irritating voice. Originally from London, Louise Haughty was one of the few people in the North East who practiced 'RP' or 'received pronunciation', which OFSTED loved, yet most of the local population actively despised.

As I arrived at the classroom, I noticed a few of the students were huddled around in a circle, screeching and flapping like a flock of excited seagulls. They were pushing and shoving each other, as though they were trying to get away from something. And then I saw it on the floor.

"Pick that up. Now, please." I tried to remain calm as I tried to comprehend the new lows they had gone to. How much more of this would I have to deal with in this job? And how many more times was I going to be told by senior management that everything was my fault, and have to constantly deal with these awful things alone?

"Naaaaar. I'm not touching that like, you joking miss?!"

"It's probably hers anyway. She's always in a right radge when she's got her period like."

"She thinks I'm touching that, she can think again like!"

I inhaled deeply and tried to remain calm. A used sanitary towel on the floor was not something that they generally teach you how to deal with during your training year. And yet, I knew that for every second that was passing and the students weren't learning, my head would be on the chopping block.

"Right. Meghan, could you go and get one of the maintenance staff please? A female, if possible? In the meantime, we can all go in and make a start," I smiled forcibly. Hopefully a caretaker would arrive quickly and this situation would be long forgotten. Unfortunately, the students had other ideas.

"Go yourself miss. It's your job. You're paid to be here. Why should I do anything when I'm not paid to come to school?" Meghan Craggs folded her arms and towered over me. My measly stature of 5 foot 1 (or 5 foot and a fag-end as my friends would often say) put me at a real disadvantage when teaching. Even at the age of 13, Meghan was just one of many students that were way taller than me. I blamed it on the amount of frozen ready meals from cheap convenience stores they probably ate at home, filled with unnatural growth hormones and mad cow disease. It was no secret that most children in this area were brought up on little more than chicken dippers and potato smiley faces. Tasty once in a while but if eaten every day, you ended up with children who couldn't sit still for 5 seconds, and looking like they were 23 instead of 13.

"Meghan, please do as I have asked or you give me no choice but to call the member of staff on duty," I warned. Every inch of me was praying that I wouldn't have to follow this threat through, although as I had been taught in her training year making empty threats was an absolute no go. Everything had to be followed through.

"Call them then! What are they gonna do? See if I care! Why is it always me that teachers pick on?" Meghan stormed off along the corridor out of sight, way too fast for me to be able to follow her and calm her down. I stood there frozen for a second; trying desperately not to allow the last positive thread I had clung on to, to slip away.

"Miss, do we not have a geography lesson today like?"

"Call yourself a teacher!"

"My dad's gonna ring up and go mental at her like."

"Total joke she is like."

Biting my lip, I ran to the computer to use the instant messaging system to call whichever unsavoury member of senior management was on duty. *Please respond quickly,* I prayed. If I did not inform them that Meghan had left the lesson and was wandering the corridors, I could be in real trouble with regards to safeguarding procedures.

No reply.

I looked at the class, who had now sat down and were chatting. I had the starter task on the board ready, but nobody was even looking at it. I could ask a student to go and inform a member of senior management about Meghan's disappearance, but who? Maybe Keegan Anderson. He was one of the rare gems who would actually occasionally write the date and title.

"Keegan, could you go just along to the management please and tell them what's happened?" I tried to hide the desperation in my voice. If Meghan was found and they hadn't been made aware, I would likely be in for a disciplinary.

"No."

"Please, Keegan."

"You can't make me."

The situation felt impossible, and I felt myself begin to tumble, like a giant landslide. First small pebbles and rocks gave way, then without warning, huge chunks of earth began to collapse. Biting my lip as I stared at the computer screen, unable to look at their surly faces, I felt a tear prick my eyelid.

Oh god no. Not in front of them. Please don't let them see.

"OH MY GOD, MISS IS *CRYING!* AAAAHAHAHAHAHA!" The glee in Ashlynn Armstrong's voice was shrill and cruel, and the majority of the class exploded with hoots and laughter.

"You alright miss?" Sneered Paige Dodds, who was clearly overjoyed at this chaotic situation. Several students hurriedly got out their phones, including Hayden Wilkinson, who began to blast a repeat recording of an American teenager guffawing "DEEEEZ NUTS."

I had had enough. I wasn't going to allow a group of 13-14 year olds make me feel miserable for any longer. I had put up with enough of this unhappiness when I myself had been at school.

"Phone, thank you Hayden." I held out my hand expectantly, reinstating control. Unfortunately, control in this hell hole dump of a school was impossible to achieve.

"You can bugger off. It's mine. You can't take my property."

"When it's interfering with my lesson and stopping people from learning, I can. You'll get it back at the end of the lesson Hayden."

"No."

My already limited supply of patience was completely depleted, and I was done arguing with this group of stubborn teenagers. Seeing a minute opportunity, I pounced and grabbed Hayden's phone as he turned to smirk at Kieran Forsyth, swooping it clean from the desk.

"What-the...AAAAAAARGHHHHH!"

I felt a blow to the side of my head, and before I could react, two hands clasped around my neck. I couldn't believe it. He was actually trying to strangle me.

"Don't you ever touch my stuff again, you horrible bitch!" roared Hayden, each word viciously accompanied by vulgar expletives which I need not repeat.

I was powerless to say or do anything. Even at the age of 14, the strength of a male was too strong to escape. I glanced desperately at the other students for a glimpse of a lifeline, yet before I lost consciousness, all I could see was indifference.

In my training year I had excelled, and had been praised for my creativity and engaging lessons, and had been described as a complete natural. In an environment where I was well supported, I thrived. In an environment where I was completely alone, I was drowning, with no-one to save me.

***

"So, it's your word against his then. Do you know what this means for the department?" Oliver Mehmet paced up and down his classroom, not even looking at me. I hadn't even been offered a glass of water following this ordeal, or god forbid, a cup of tea.

"Why didn't you send him to me?"

I hadn't said much until now, but I was ready for the blame game, and I was about to snap. "I didn't think I needed to. I shouldn't be wrong for confiscating a phone that was disrupting my lesson!"

Oliver looked up, probably about to reply with something ridiculous, when Claire Turner and Suzanne Powell strode into the classroom. Although they were marginally nicer than Jessica and Debbie they were still senior management, and not to be trusted with a barge pole. In fact, they usually held the barge pole for beating you with when you were down.

"So, we hear there's been an incident. And there's been an allegation made against you. Quite a serious one, too. Did you hit Hayden Wilkinson?"

My mouth fell open.

"*WHAT?!* But he just strangled me! He could have killed me! All just because I took his phone! Ask any of the other students, they'll tell you what happened! Why aren't you expelling him, or at least suspending him right this second?!"

"Because at the moment it seems that his voice is louder than yours, Lilee. We have no choice but to suspend you pending a full investigation, with the potential involvement of the police if necessary. And he is a looked-after child, which makes this case even more serious."

Shaking with hot fury, I wobbled as I stood. I couldn't get out of there fast enough, yet my legs weren't working as quickly as I needed them to. The stern and unkind faces followed me to the bathroom, where I hastily threw up my morning coffee, heaving and retching, hot tears smarting down my face which felt ten years older than just a year ago. I couldn't believe that I had begrudgingly followed my mother's advice to 'make something of myself', getting into almost sixty thousand pounds worth of debt from student loans and overdrafts, and this was the result. Surely this couldn't be the remainder of my adult life. "I'd rather work in McDonald's," I thought furiously, bitter with regret for having wasted the last year being completely miserable, terrified to accept that the choice I had made may not have been the right one.

I couldn't help but think, what on earth was Daniel going to make of all this?

Still shaking with fury and disbelief, I staggered outside to the car, almost unable to grasp the door handle because I was shaking so much. I felt like my entire body was experiencing the aftershock of an earthquake measuring magnitude 9 on the Richter scale, and my stomach was the epicentre. I had to call someone.

"Hello? What's the matter?" My friend, Sally, answered the phone after just two rings. She was now unfortunately quite used to these spontaneous SOS phone calls.

As I began to spatter away the day's events, I absentmindedly swung the steering wheel round too far to reverse, not thinking or concentrating at all.

Crunch.

Ohhhhhh *NO NO NOOOOO!* I wailed, head in my palms. I had, in my moment of absolute stupidity, reversed the car in an almost 180 degree turn and rammed straight into the side door of another teacher's parked car. It had crumpled like tin foil. Leaving a note under the wiper wouldn't be enough, and I couldn't just drive off as the car park had CCTV in order to track down any escaping students. I was going to have to go back into the lair of the dragons of senior management and admit what I had just done. I just hoped and prayed that the car didn't belong to Jessica or Debbie. I reluctantly looked again at the damaged vehicle and saw that it wasn't an Audi or a BMW, but a Vauxhall Corsa. It could belong to a member of admin staff or a teaching assistant, I mused.

I dashed into reception, though the hurried pace was only due to the sudden downpour of icy cold rain. Talk about icing on top of the cake.

"I've just hit a car outside..." I mumbled with utmost embarrassment, waiting for the jokes to begin at my expense. They didn't. Instead, the receptionist glanced up at me and gave a small smile.

"Ah, no way. Happens to us all. Did you get which registration number it was and I can find out who the owner is?"

"It's Mrs Powell's!" rasped Tony, the caretaker, who had obviously seen and heard what had been happening and was ambling towards us. Tony was a nice man, who you could tell enjoyed a few too many pints down the local most evenings, owing to his ruddy complexion and his very out of shape physique. Still, I imagined that changing the toilet roll and operating the hoover daily was not overly strenuous, and so his job was a suitable match for his lifestyle.

I had hit Suzanne Powell's car. Senior management's favourite. I felt my stomach slip through my legs and plummet right down to the core of planet earth. I would have much preferred to have hit a member of the royal family during a jubilee parade with the whole world watching, than Suzanne Powell's car. The woman who had just looked at me straight in the eyes and likely discarded my entire career in a matter of seconds without even a drop of sympathy or remorse.

"Tell her to call me and that I'll pay for the damage, that I'm really really sorry, and that I didn't mean it..." I babbled as I grabbed my keys and dashed out of the school once again. I didn't give the school a second look as I shot out of there like a bat out of hell, jumped into the car and left the car park as fast as possible, pushing the Juke to its limits down the country roads and wondering whether I should just crash it at 60 miles an hour into the nearest wall and end this nightmare that was my life.

I returned to an empty house and did what I now believe no-one should ever do once they have left work for the day and checked my emails. As usual, my inbox was already brimming with irate e-mails from my 'mentor' Oliver Mehmet, which according to him, were supposed to 'help' me. Once you have completed your teacher training in England, your first year as a qualified teacher known as your NQT (Newly Qualified Teacher) year, and your progress is monitored by a fellow teacher within your department who acts as a 'mentor'. I'm still pretty sure that he got 'mentor' and 'dementor' confused when reading the job description.

He certainly sucked all of the happiness out of me just like the scary hooded figures in the Harry Potter series did. The
e-mails often went back and forward until around 10pm when he went to bed, and tonight was unfortunately no exception. They were usually complaints of something I hadn't done right at some point during the day, like not having books out on the desks ready for the students, or having a seating plan that was ineffective. I would reply stating the obvious, that having 36 students in a class, two thirds of which were identified as having additional needs, would render any seating plan ineffective, and then he would reply saying if I wasn't cut out for this job then I shouldn't do it.

He would also often share complaints made about me by other members of staff or senior management and pressurise me, saying things like: 'Debbie said she wasn't happy with what she saw on her 'learning walk' when she visited your classroom today. As your mentor, if you go down, I go down. And then the whole department goes down. May I remind you that you have to think of others as well as yourself?"

Tonight's attack was particularly savage. His insults of my incompetence and his total lack of concern for how I was feeling after today's events burned my eyes and I wondered in desperation how I had managed to establish myself in such a harsh environment, where I had no allies whatsoever to rely on in the time of a crisis, just nonchalant robots with hearts as cold as the local climate in winter.

If I could go back in time, I would have slammed the lid of the laptop shut and realised what was happening here, but the curiosity and the belief that there was indeed something terribly wrong with me kept me glued to the screen. I had even sent screenshots of Oliver's emotionally paralysing e-mails to my friend Sally who had told me that this was bullying, and I had to leave and get out of that school, but I couldn't do it for the fear of proving him right. According to him I was 'going down' and 'wasn't cut out for it'. I was so desperate to prove Oliver Mehmet and the senior management wrong, but at what cost?

This had gone on for way too long and it had got to the point where his voice was constantly swirling around my head, telling me over and over again that I was a failure, a disappointment, no good for anything, a burden, a waste of space, everyone else was better than me and I should have given up a long time ago, and whose classes were nothing but a chain of debacles and fiascos which ruined everything for everyone. Ultimately, when you are constantly faced with those who are so unkind, it only takes some time before you start believing their words as your own.

My mind and vision blurred from overwhelming despair and my eyes swimming with red wine, I turned over a box of diazepam tablets in my hand, that the doctor had prescribed a couple of months ago to help me relax on planes.

Tuesday, 20th October 2015
Gateshead, Tyne and Wear, England

When Daniel returned at around two in the morning following a long shift at Nissan, he was ready for a nice cold beer before bed. He too had had a tough day, and had watched one of his colleagues break down as the company handed out yet another redundancy. Instead Daniel walked through the door to the cat Zizou Wazizi who was mewling ferociously. Although he was very used to the annoying and slightly murderous zig-zagging through his legs, he noticed that this behaviour even for Zizou Wazizi, was extreme. He followed her through to the living room to find me slumped lifelessly on the sofa, my face blotchy with angst and exhaustion. He touched my arm and in alarm found it to be ice cold. I don't remember what went through my mind that night, only that I just wanted everything to stop.

<u>Chapter two:</u> it's just a cat

Friday, 23rd October 2015
Gateshead, Tyne & Wear, England

"I'm fine thanks. Honestly..."
I was so tempted to hang up the phone to avoid the steady flow of calls of family and friends. In this

scenario, it is always possible to divide the callers into two groups: those who are genuinely worried, and those who just want to know the gossip. I wasn't sure which one was worse.

Some of my friends had foreseen this, and knew all too well how unhappy I had become within the past couple of years. I had been very grateful especially to my friend Sally who had phoned constantly to check that I was alright, although I knew it must have been excruciatingly tedious for her, having to listen again and again to the complaints of a day in the life of a teacher at Panaculty Academy.

My mum had taken the news the worst, and I was racked with guilt and worry whether this could push her over the edge again, however my mother's continuous on-off battle with depression and life in general had made her strong. She was a seasoned nurse, and had previously worked nightshift in a palliative care hospice caring for patients dying of cancer. Working nightshift alone was enough for most people, but dealing with death and loss on a daily basis for so many years had taken its toll. On top of all this, there had been the extremely messy divorce from Jeremy, my father, back in 2004, which had been far from simple. But that's another story entirely.

A couple of days on I was feeling just as bad, if not even worse as I had when I had tried to end it all on Monday evening. On top of hating my life and just wanting to disappear into thin air, I now also felt guilty at having upset the people closest to me. When I had come round, groggy and numb, before the realisation of "oh great, I'm still alive" hit me, my first sight was of Daniel sitting next to me. He couldn't even look at me and when I had asked him how long I had been there, he just shrugged coldly, rose from his seat and swiftly walked out of the room. Though a flood of family and friends arrived soon after, meaning that he must have contacted them to say that I was alright, he didn't return.

I couldn't blame him at all, and I knew how it felt; that feeling of abandonment, how someone could even think about putting their loved ones through so much pain. I had resented my mother for the most part of my teenage years because of her frequent suicide threats, her overwhelming unhappiness with her life, and her anger at me deciding to continue speaking to my father. She would drink too much, become hysterical, and she would never listen to me. Although the older and wiser me now would have dealt with it all much better, the younger and temperamental me back then couldn't at the time. After my parents divorced, I moved away to live with my grandparents in Newcastle where I could start afresh, far away from where I grew up near Doncaster and where I would have to endure constant reminders of the dysfunctional situation we had all found ourselves in.

Mum's method of dealing with all that had happened was to hit the bottle, and so she became extremely difficult to reason with. When I talked to grandma one night about mum's suicide letters and vicious outbursts, she responded with much less alarm than I had anticipated. "She's been doing that since she was 18 pet, don't worry. She was born on a Wednesday after all. Wednesday's child is full of woe and all that!" Grandma was always full of wise sayings, though I never was sure that referring to the 'Monday's child' nursery rhyme was a sufficient explanation nor solution for the gaping wounds which had scarred my mother's emotional well-being.

Monday's child is fair of face,
Tuesday's child is full of grace,
Wednesday's child is full of woe,
Thursday's child has far to go.
Friday's child is loving and giving,
Saturday's child works hard for a living,
But the child who is born on the Sabbath day,
is bonny and blithe and good and gay.

Whenever I mentioned that I was living with my grandparents, people would react with sympathy as they automatically assumed something had gone terribly wrong. Something had gone terribly wrong of course, but they didn't need to know that. I was in fact over the moon at the prospect of living with my grandparents; I had always enjoyed a very special and close relationship with my dear grandma from as early as I can remember. She was a wonderfully good natured woman who was so forgiving, patient and loving. The day before I was due to start at Newcastle College, I was nervous as I wouldn't know anybody. My cousins in the area hadn't lifted a finger once I had moved up there as I thought they would have done. Grandma had simply said,

"well pet, if you smile and are friendly to people, you usually find they will smile and be friendly back." It was very plain, but very sound advice. I was excited to enjoy 'cheese dreams,' which was my grandma's speciality snack – a cheese sandwich, dunked in beaten egg and fried. My granddad's version was cheese on toast, though by the time he would make it he was usually so drunk he would put the whole block of cheese on the toast under the grill. As a devout cheese lover, I certainly never complained. Whenever the band 'dire straits' came on the radio, they would dance together in the kitchen without a care in the world. These memories will seem so simple to anyone else, though I would do anything to relive those moments with them again.

I pretty much made friends as soon as I arrived at the central train station in Newcastle. The workers at Costa coffee told me to wait until their shift ended and we would hit the pubs. It was totally mad and spontaneous, and I loved it. Getting away and making a new start had been the best thing. It hadn't taken me long at all to settle into my new home, reinvent myself, and make a good circle of friends at college. After about six months, all of a sudden one day, mum showed up on the doorstep of grandma and granddad's house - a modest two up, two down semi-detached house in Whitley Bay — as though nothing had happened, and then tried to re-impose her parental authority on me, just like that. This didn't work at all, and resulted in many unpleasant clashes right up until I left for University. The whole episode was just absolute chaos. Although it does sound awful, literally nothing bothered me anymore. Becoming numb to such events was the only way to deal with them without going insane yourself. But now here I was. Repeating the same misery as my mother. The phone rang again and I answered after two rings, knowing already who it was. It had taken a long time, but once I had gone away to university my visits to see mum were much less frequent. Therefore, the time we spent together became more valued and special and gradually we were able to form that mother and daughter bond that each of us had wanted all along. Better late than never.

"This was your cry for help. You cannot keep going on like this. You have to get out of that school, and change your life. Don't go back after the October half term. Use this week to decide what you're going to do," said mum. She was saying what I already knew, and I knew that I had to make a fresh start somewhere totally new, but what about Daniel? We had rented a house together, got a cat together and everything. Real grown up stuff.

"You know what I want to do. I've always wanted to go abroad. But Daniel won't ever leave his family. We've talked about it loads of times. It's out of the question."

Mum sighed and paused for a moment, before adding, "If he loves you, and you love him, it will all work out somehow." This was the best piece of advice I had heard for a while. It was almost like someone had waved a checked white and black 'go!' flag. I flipped open my laptop and typed fast. I hovered over the international job advert section on the Times Education website, and was surprised and thrilled to see there were already postings advertised for teachers of modern languages in Hong Kong, Beijing, Vietnam, Mexico, and Sri Lanka. I applied to all and left my destiny to the hands of fate. My mum was right. Daniel would surely understand.

Sunday, 8th November 2015
Killingworth, North Tyneside, England

"So you're moving to Sri Lanka? What are you going to do there?" Daniel's mum Maureen made no effort to hide her concern and disapproval at all at this news, as she busied herself in the kitchen preparing the Sunday dinner. Although she was far from my favourite person, she was an extremely good cook. Getting tasty food was literally the only thing that made the weekly obligatory visits to Daniel's parental home bearable, and even then 'bearable' was pushing it. Usually suffering from the after effects of a Saturday night out with friends, I had to endure the ear splitting screams of 10 terribly behaved grandchildren, who were the result of Daniel's sister's incessant desire to breed as though the human race was an endangered species.

I had found out the previous Wednesday that I had got the job that I had applied for at Thambili international school, one of the leading international schools in Sri Lanka. I had been very surprised that instead of the gruelling full day interview and numerous forms I had had to complete in the UK for a teaching job, for this school a 20 minute chat over Skype with the head teacher and the school's registrar had been sufficient. Following the interview, I had received an e-mail with the offer of a contract later that day, which I had hastily printed, signed, and posted off to Sri Lanka the very same day. Admittedly it was a country that I knew quite little about, as generally in UK mainstream schools the countries which you extensively study about in Geography are always the same: Bangladesh for flooding, Brazil for shanty towns and Japan for earthquakes.

"I'll find something there. I'm excited for the adventure anyway. You know how I hate Nissan." Daniel offered the same reply to his mum as he would continue to repeat over and over again in the coming months. It was only November, and I wasn't due to begin my job until the next academic year, so we would be flying out in August the following year in 2016. His reassurance was never enough for Maureen however, and she would continuously whine about how he would miss his nieces and nephews growing up, and how he would be so far away in her annoying whiny high pitched voice. I became used to just ignoring her now, and my friends would all be prepared for the barrage of messages that would come through on a Sunday afternoon when I desperately needed to talk to someone normal to regain my sanity in that house. Suddenly, I heard words which grabbed my attention like a loud and striking clap of thunder.

"If you're married, it will be much easier for you to go."

Married? I cringed at the word. It stood for everything I hated, no freedom and 'settling down.' I had been quite happy with just cohabiting, and was one of those who felt strongly that a marriage certificate was just a piece of paper and a huge waste of money for just one day, which usually ended up being tailored to everyone else's wishes and needs, rather those of the actual couple getting married. Though I hated to admit it however, I had a feeling that Maureen was right. After all, maybe it was just my own reservations about marriage that were the problem. Daniel had been a good partner: we cooked together, laughed together, holidayed together, drank together, and could tell each other everything. He had always been good to me, so surely getting married wouldn't be so bad, and a sensible thing to do for the long term, especially if we were to then relocate somewhere else after my two year contract was up in Sri Lanka. Maybe we would end up somewhere with stricter laws where we would probably have to be married anyway, like Saudi Arabia or Brunei.

Although I didn't have a great deal of time to make up my mind about getting married, there was one thing that I certainly was sure of, which was handing in my resignation to that god awful school. As I was a teacher of three different subjects, I wasn't sure that my resignation letter would be received well, though it was something I definitely had to do for my own well-being and sanity. As soon as we arrived back at our house in Gateshead, I hurriedly punched out the first resignation letter that I had ever written, requesting that my final day be the last day before breaking up for the Christmas holidays. Despite the fact that teachers were usually required to give a full term's notice before leaving, I hoped that the head teacher would understand. If anything, he would probably be pleased – after all, I had constantly been reminded by members of the senior management that I was nothing more than a burden, and brought little to the school. I e-mailed it to myself so that I could print it out at school tomorrow morning. I was due to return back after having had three weeks off work – two weeks signed off on the sick, or at least that was what I would tell any future employer rather than divulge what had happened on that awful Monday afternoon in October. One week had been the scheduled week long half term break. I wasn't sure what I was going to do for the seven months after the Christmas holidays for work before I flew out to Sri Lanka in August, but I would find something. I had a secure job now anyway, so anything would do to fill the gap. There were still a couple of months left to get something arranged for the first half of 2016. As if someone had actually read my thoughts, my phone suddenly sprang to life and reminded me of its existence. It was a number calling that I did not recognise. I answered.

"Hello Lilee, its Ajwad – do you remember me from the PE department? I left some time ago and now I'm working for a company called Capita. Instead of teaching, I recruit teachers now. Are you still at the same school?"

"I've literally just written my resignation letter," I replied quickly. This was unravelling into a very worthwhile phone conversation. I thought that I heard Ajwad stifle a laugh at the other end, but I couldn't be sure. I had never known Ajwad that well; just that he had been the head of the PE department, and rumour had it, that he had faced multiple allegations and attacks from parents, who were adamant that he had made sexual comments aimed at two 15 year old girls in Year 10. I did not know the truth, nor would I ever discover it for real, though I knew that when someone had written 'filfy paki' and 'go home u dirty immagrunt' in permanent marker on Ajwad's windscreen, the students had been identified, but pretty much nothing had happened in the way of punishment. The town in which the school was located was a big EDL stronghold (English defence league, an extreme right wing group) and the senior management would rather let the children get away with hate crimes for fear of the parents' reactions.

To my knowledge, Ajwad had been born and raised in Newcastle, the son of Kuwaiti parents who had settled in the North East during the Iraqi invasion of Kuwait and had worked hard to become respected members of the community. Ajwad spoke with a warm and strong Geordie accent, yet sadly, being from a Middle Eastern background, he was still a target for those who one can refer to as 'gammons': white people who turn an unhealthy shade of puce when getting angry about political issues, particularly when discussing immigration.

I remembered the time when I had found a really interesting video on Newsround about young Afghani children, playing football and talking about their dreams and ambitions for the future. I had wanted to show my Year 9 tutor group one morning, though both senior management and the other members of the language department forbade it. When I had protested that they should at least give it a try, their response was that they were all too busy to clear up yet another of my messes.

"When are you available to start at a different school? I have lots of posts here in nice schools – ranging from supply for just a day, or a longer contract. For example, I have this really great school, but it's a bit far away... could you come into the Newcastle office tomorrow and we can have a chat? We're open until 5.45, so that should be plenty of time for you to get down here after you finish school," Ajwad had answered my question before I could even ask it, though I was already trying not to think about school the next day.

"As it's my first day back, I should manage to get out a bit earlier than normal. Look forward to seeing you again!" I hung up, and the thought of what state the books would be in crept into my mind.

I was unable to sleep that Sunday night, my stomach crunching with nerves and anxiety at the thought of stepping back into that den of evil the following day. I was also giddy with excitement at the thought of seeing Ajwad in the evening. It was still two full terms away until Daniel and I were due to fly out to Sri Lanka in August, and maybe because of him they might actually be bearable. Though I was unsure. If the senior management had been right, I was not cut out to be a teacher at all, and should basically just curl up and die and rid the world of my presence.

Frustrated at being unable to sleep, I went downstairs and decided to make myself a cup of tea, and wait for Daniel to come back from his late shift. His shifts at

Nissan would alternate between late shifts and night shifts, so he would either arrive home at around two in the morning had he been on a late shift, or eight in the morning if he had been on a night shift. This meant that often, we were like ships passing in the night and would barely ever see each other through the week. By the time he would get home from work, I would be either asleep or have left for work already.

A few of our friends had pointed out that this pattern given my struggle at work was unhealthy, and that me coming home to an empty house certainly was not helping matters. I had always said that it was fine as there was always the cat, Zizou Wazizi for company. She was a beautiful little thing, light grey with a white bib and a little pink wet nose. Many had commented that she was not normal for a cat and more like a dog, as whenever I returned from work she would run to the door with her tail wagging. She would frequently curl around my head like a small furry pillow as I slept, and there was certainly no need for an alarm clock in the morning. If anybody's toes were sticking out of the bottom of the duvet, 'hunt the toe' was unfortunately Zizou Wazizi's favourite game, and despite many efforts to alter this, nothing had sufficed as effective enough to curb the kitty's bloodthirsty and irrational enthusiasm for human phalanges.

Speaking of Zizou Wazizi, where was she?

The door opened with a crack, and in walked Daniel, covered in oil and grease as always. I had hoped that Zizou Wazizi would follow him meowing irritably, but nothing.

"What are you still doing up at this time?"
"Couldn't sleep. Did you see Zizou? I haven't seen her since... I haven't seen her today at all," I realised, a familiar pool of dread forming in the pit of my stomach. It was not like Zizou to be gone for this long, maybe a couple of hours at the very most usually. Something wasn't right.

Daniel didn't even need to ask anything. From the look on my face he got it straightaway.
"I'll go and look for her," he said hurriedly. The poor man hadn't even had chance to take off his jacket. The minutes that subsequently passed by felt like hours. Painful hours. The same thoughts whirled around in my head as I prayed to a God I didn't believe in: *please, don't let anything have happened to her. Let her come home safe and annoying and sweet as always. She's only a year old, she has so much more life to live, it isn't fair to take it away now...*

I couldn't just sit and do nothing. I should have gone with Daniel. I quickly opened Facebook and posted a message in the Gateshead area lost and found pets group. At this time, it was very unlikely that anyone would see my post now, but at least it was out there, and people could look for her. Maybe she had just fancied an adventure, and she had grown tired and bored of 3 Grove Terrace. I hoped that no-one had decided to keep her as their own, though I couldn't blame them if they had; she was unique, special, beautiful and adorable; wonderful in every way. Why had I always complained about Zizou's meowing and toe swiping? I would take a million days of it if only she could be back here now.

This wasn't the first time we had gone through worry with Zizou Wazizi. When she was just weeks old, shortly after Daniel had first brought Zizou home, I had still been in York, finishing up my teacher training. She had jumped into a scolding hot bath which Daniel had ran, when he had gone downstairs to watch TV for 15 minutes as the bath cooled down slightly. He had returned upstairs to find a lifeless ball of grey at the bottom of the bath and phoned me panicking and swearing, only for little Zizou to cough up the water and scratch Daniel to ribbons in a furious rage.

He had rushed her to the vets as quickly as he could, and had been told by the young Scottish vet that her 'wee nipples' were burnt, and as she was so young it was unlikely she would make it through. Zizou spent the night in an oxygen tank and under close supervision, and amazingly by the next morning she was right as rain, eating and playing. Daniel had nearly fainted when the vet had told them how much the oxygen tank cost per hour. It had happened so soon after the adoption that we hadn't even had time to organise any pet insurance for her. Money didn't matter when it came to Zizou though. She was worth it.

Suddenly, a ping brought me out of my reverie. Someone had replied to my Facebook post. My hands shaking with nervous anticipation, I clicked on the notification, expecting to read that Zizou was safe and well, harassing someone else and eating all their food, and that she could come home now. But that wasn't what I read.

A local policewoman had replied, saying that on her evening shift she had seen a small grey cat on the road, matching Zizou Wazizi's description exactly. Like Daniel she must have not long finished her shift. She had sent over her number via private message and said to phone her as soon as possible. Daniel returned empty handed, also looking worried, and I was grateful for his company, as I instinctively knew deep down that this phone call was not going to be a pleasant one and I was going to need a shoulder to cry on after this. I dialled the number, and though embarrassed as I was I could not hold back the tears as Michelle the kind policewoman, confirmed the awful news which felt like a clasp around my neck which choked me.

Monday, 9th November 2015
Gateshead, Tyne and Wear, England

"It's just a cat. You've had enough time off as it is. We've all had to work twice as hard." Oliver Mehmet's voice was cold, harsh, and unforgiving, and though he was speaking on the phone, I could see his thick eyebrows knitting together in fury, his fists clenching.

"Please," I begged, fresh tears in my eyes. "I'm really not up to it... I can't deal with the students if they're difficult today, I really don't have the energy." Every word I was saying was true; I really couldn't stop crying over my little Zizou's death. The words of my 'mentor' echoed painfully in my ears. *It's just a cat.* Were these people even human, or robots? Or was there something wrong with me? If Zizou was just a cat, and not worth getting upset over, then why was learning of the untimely death of such a loving and innocent being so painful?

"Louise didn't take any time off when her dog died. Do you know what? Just do whatever you want. The head teacher will speak to you about your conduct I'm sure." I really wanted to say, *'Louise doesn't have a heart, which is probably why she felt no emotion when her dog died and is an abyss of nothingness,'* but Oliver had hung up the phone.

I knew if I didn't go into school, there would be big trouble and I really wasn't in a position to lose money or any more sleep. I tried to hold on to the two positive events that would be occurring that day, the handing in of my resignation letter and my meeting with Ajwad later in the evening.

Reluctantly and with a heavy heart, I chugged some leftover red wine, hoping it would numb the overwhelming dread, brushed my teeth savagely, grabbed my bag and set off on the short journey to school. I had made sure to dress well, given that I would be having an informal interview later on. I was soon to learn that over the half term break there had been numerous additions of supply staff recruited from Capita, the very same recruitment company for which Ajwad worked: Darius Papadopoulos in RE (religious education), Albert Stanton in English, Gaynor Smith - a new teaching assistant (hurrah!) and dozens of supply teachers in an attempt to balance the rapidly collapsing science and maths departments. In pure desperation, the school had even outsourced from the military; the new Head of Year 10 – George Monroe, a Scotsman who was not a teacher, but a corporal in the army for many years. A well-made and necessary appointment.

The only department in the school which had ever displayed any kind of miniscule success was the humanities department, which had previously been led by Kerry Collins, a wonderful, quirky, flower loving hippy, who had inspired the students with photographs of her yearly travels to Thailand. Sadly, she had left the previous term for pastures new, and had been the only real source of support or positivity for me during my fledgling year. The students at Panaculty Academy enjoyed History especially, as they could freely share their hatred of Margaret Thatcher who was the fiercely seen as the antichrist in the region.

Having a few new faces around was a breath of fresh air; Albert Stanton was a very experienced teacher and fellow linguist, and having taught in several international schools around the world, he had a wealth of advice and knowledge which I was eager to hear, if I could get a spare few minutes. Darius Papadopoulos was a young, yet extremely educated individual, hailing originally from Greece, before relocating to London to complete his PHD in something very interesting and philosophical sounding.

Having handed in my resignation letter at the first possible opportunity to reception, I hurriedly introduced myself in the first floor 'staff pod' before placing some milk in the fridge for my coffee when I had a couple of spare minutes. There was no communal staffroom, but six separate 'staff pods', as it was widely discussed; 'divide and conquer' was clearly the management's tactic to crush any possibility of rebellion. I had the pleasure of the wonderful Year 8 Set 3 class to start the day with, yet with a promising evening ahead I felt ready for them, like a medieval knight ready for the bloodthirsty opposition to come running over the hill for battle. They were going to sit down, shut up, and respond to every single comment I had ever written in their books that they hadn't even bothered to read. Then the senior management would come in and be in ecstasy at the outstanding marking and feedback that lay before their eyes. No-one was going to ruin this fool proof plan. No-one at all unless they wished to end up in detention for the rest of their lives.

As I switched on the computer and opened up my usual bombardment of e-mails, I clicked on the top one which was in the unread folder.
The headteacher will see you in his office at 9.40am.
Oh no. I knew exactly what it would be about, and as the head teacher almost never left his office unless it was to have his photograph taken, I had no idea what to expect. Still, I knew that the feeling of relief was on the way, but not here quite yet. As I heard the bell ring, and the subsequent cacophony of the Year 8's thundering down the corridor towards my classroom, I remembered what happened in Lord of the Rings when the fellowship of the ring were surrounded by orcs; they fought valiantly and they won. And that was exactly what I was going to do this morning. Fight and win, although not physically of course.

After five minutes of the usual grumbling and complaining, bums were on seats and students had at least opened their French books and glanced at the questions which they were to respond to, yet the inevitable flood of questions washed in like a tidal wave.

"What does add another adjective mean? What are connectives? I don't know what intensifiers are. What do you mean when you say justify your opinion?"

The worst was the long repetitive drawl of "I don't get iiiiiiit."

This was exactly the problem. They didn't 'get' anything except Snapchat stories or likes on Instagram.

Blooms taxonomy may work well in a private school, but not somewhere like this, where children come in on inflated literacy grades so the primary teachers can go up the pay scale, leaving the poor secondary school teachers to attempt to make up the short fall. 'Blooms taxonomy' is a system created in 1956, which shows exactly how out dated it is, by the educational psychologist Benjamin Bloom. It has caused a major headache for teachers throughout the UK, yet has been a gift from the gods for senior management, who can use this as a tool to manipulate their minions even further. At Panaculty Academy, the members of senior management would conduct their weekly book scrutiny, to inspect whether teachers had been using the words highlighted in this pyramid of pointlessness in their marking in relation to the ability of the student.

Bloom's Taxonomy

Create	Formulate, investigate
Evaluate	Appraise, critique
Analyse	Contrast, compare

Apply	Execute, implement
Understand	Classify, discuss, explain
Remember	Define, duplicate

On the SIMS data system, which is used in most schools in the UK many of these children had arrived in Year 7 with data supplied from their primary schools assuring us that they were working at a level 4 or 5. However most of them could barely read and write. I recalled the time last year when I had asked them who had read a book recently. Only two students of a class of 34 raised their hand.

What senior management frankly refused to understand was that these children did not understand words that were even at the very bottom of the pyramid, such as 'duplicate, classify, or execute'. I had repeatedly told them that marking in this way, especially when it comes to languages, was absolutely not accessible for these children. And of course, when they inevitably could not respond to the feedback, they would become frustrated and kick off. I would then somehow have to deal with the shambles with absolutely no support. Despite many indignant conversations with the gargoyles of senior management, they would not change their tack, and would just repeat like broken robots who could not listen: "Are their books beautiful? Have you followed the marking policy? Have you used blooms taxonomy?" Unfortunately they weren't robots, and they did not simply have a circuit board that you could just rip out to make them stop.

Suddenly, a low roar erupted from the other end of the corridor. For perhaps the first ever time, the students sat bolt upright instead of their usual slouch in absolute silence, ears on end, craning their necks in desperation to hear what was happening.

I recognised that sound. It was the sound of a teacher who had absolutely lost it. In this school, it was sadly a rather frequent noise.

Shinade Crawley, a Year 7 student, burst into the classroom, breathless, yet somehow still managing to reel off the hot gossip at a thousand miles per hour. "Oh my god miss, Mr Poppadoppawoppa – can't say his name - has smashed up the classroom and he slammed the keyboard against the wall and all the little keys even pinged out and one nearly hit Kieran in the eye and - he proper yelled at us like! He reet scared us ye knaaaa!"

I really wanted to say, 'you all probably deserved it and I hope you're scared! HA!' but of course I couldn't say that. This had been Mr Papadopoulos' first day. The poor man. Though he did have the advantage of being on supply, so he could walk out and leave at any time he liked, and did not have to adhere to the school's ridiculous 'beautiful books' policy or slightly disturbing obsession with data. Supply staff were also much better paid than teachers on a contract, and they had way less responsibility or stress. No planning or marking or bullying by senior management! I knew exactly how this meeting tonight with Ajwad was going to go before it had even happened. Supply teaching was definitely the answer.

<u>Chapter 3</u> – The Haggerty inspection

Tuesday, 5th January 2016
Newton Aycliffe, County Durham, England

The New Year had brought a new lease of life. As good as his word, Ajwad had matched me to fill an urgent vacancy for a teacher of geography at a school an hour's commute away, and although I was apprehensive at having to drive down the A1 every morning and afternoon in rush hour, Ajwad assured me that it would be worth it. It was.

Haggerty Academy was set at the back of a council estate in Easington Colliery which was a very similar location to where Panaculty Academy had been, an old pit mining community, devastated by Maggie Thatcher and her ruthless Tory government. Both schools housed the offspring of many second or third generation claimants of benefits, given little choice given the system. The main problem of such areas was that people rarely valued education or employment anymore, as usually people would be financially better off on benefits than they would be had they worked and paid taxes. Therefore, the attitude in these deprived communities had very quickly become 'what's the point?' By closing the industry which had been the heartbeat of the north east region, there remained bitter and isolated communities, which were now fuelled by teenage pregnancies and alcohol.

Kirsten Fortune, the head teacher of Haggerty Academy was a remarkable woman, and had also previously been a French specialist. What she lacked in height she made up for in strong leadership, and silence would fall as soon as she walked into the staffroom. She was firm but fair, and was always out and about in the corridors, rarely just sat in her office as the head teacher at Panaculty Academy had done. It often took me a long time to gain respect for authoritarian figures, however Mrs Fortune had it instantly.

As I waited gingerly in the staffroom for Jakub Kaminski, the head of geography, I felt a much more positive vibe about this place. At 8.55, just five minutes before the bell was due to ring, I heard a screech of freshly polished shoes colliding with the vinyl floor, and a whirlwind of a bald headed man wrapped in a trendy beige trench coat bustling through the door towards me.

"Sorry I'm late. Was test driving the new Nissan Leaf and the bloody thing ran out of charge," panted Jakub. "Being a geography teacher and all that...thought I might as well give it a try. But I live a bit too far away and me girlfriend's house is even further..." He spoke with a strong Teesside accent, and I was pleased to see that my new boss was, much unlike that foul bitter piece of misery Louise had been, young; early thirties at the most. And down to earth – excellent! I much preferred down to earth people over those who were nit-picky.

Jakub handed me a copy of my timetable, and informed me that I would also have a year 7 tutor group. "Sorry I didn't get it e-mailed over to you sooner. Holidays...you know..." I didn't mind. I also learned that I was actually filling the position of Kerry Collins, who had managed to escape the deathly clutches of Panaculty Academy before me. She had stayed just one term before moving to Greece at the drop of a hat once her husband had found a job there. Living and working abroad had always been in Kerry's heart. Although it made me happy that Kerry had also been welcomed here, I knew that Mrs Collin's boots would be pretty big to fill.

My Year 7 class were a mixed and lively bunch – Charity, whose mother I learned, was from the traveller community, and had ran away with a man from the Caribbean, who was Charity's father. I really respected people like that, who broke the mould and went with their heart. There was also Helen, who was as tall as a 16 year old at least, and although she towered over her peers, I would soon learn that her heart was as large as her height. There was Euan, whose sister was in a wheelchair, suffering from multiple sclerosis. There was Jayden, whose father was in prison, leaving behind a struggling single mother and a very frustrated and angry little boy. There was also Shanice, who looked at least three years her senior and refused to wear her school uniform properly. I liked the enthusiasm of this class and how they would confidently share their opinions and talk at length about almost any topic.

For the next eight weeks I made the hour long journey without complaint to Haggerty Academy. Although I was only technically on a supply contract, I slotted in to the Humanities department and got on very well with the other staff. I taught 26 lessons a week which was pretty much the same as it had been at Panaculty Academy, but having the lessons already planned out as an array of PowerPoint's and Word documents in weekly order was extremely helpful, and the workload was now at least manageable. As a supply teacher I was not required to mark the books either, though out of loyalty to the school and my colleagues, I did. Haggerty Academy was due to have an Ofsted inspection and I knew that books 'showing progress over time' were one of the main things that the inspectors would look at.

Wednesday, 2nd March 2016
Newton Aycliffe, County Durham, England

And they did. Once the rumour "we've had the call!" had circled around the entire school like wildfire, an emergency after school meeting was announced, and the entire staff flocked to the staffroom like gaggling geese, panicking and squawking, worried about the ridiculous amount of totally unnecessary paperwork they would now have to complete. All of these teachers, many with families, would be up until stupid o' clock tonight, sacrificing their sleep uniquely for the pleasure of the inspectors, such as seating plans annotated with various jargon, lesson plans which were explained as clear as crystal, and progress data of the students. All this so they could sit and judge your entire career from watching twenty minutes of your teaching.

Kirsten Fortune, the head teacher spoke very warmly and positively during the meeting.
"We *are* a good school. Just come in, do your jobs as you normally do, and show them who we are." I left feeling determined that I would not let this remarkable woman down, who had breathed some life back into my soul, and my colleagues who had made me feel so welcome, even though I would be leaving once the school found a permanent geography teacher. Being at Haggerty Academy had helped me remember why I was passionate about teaching, and that despite the heavy workload I could do it. Despite this new found positivity the impending visit from Ofsted brought a sense of foreboding. It was almost as though I had a sixth sense.

That evening, I did not eat. I did not have time to do such things. I began to work as soon as I got home at around six, and stayed up until two in the morning, making sure that every minute detail about my students was anointed on the seating plans of all of my classes. Fortunately by this time I knew them all well. I had six lessons back to back the following day, and so the probability of an inspector entering my classroom was very high. I did not, and would not go to bed until I knew that each and every lesson was planned to perfection.

Each activity had to have at least three different tasks, (bronze, silver, and gold) to show that it was differentiated to suit students of lower, middle, and higher ability. I also had to ensure that each activity was highly engaging and interactive, and would challenge the pupils of higher ability sufficiently, as well as be accessible for the less able students. The objective and success criteria of the lesson had to be clear and achievable, and there had to be plenty of opportunities where I could demonstrate evidence of progress and assessment in the lesson. I had to make sure that there were elements of literacy and numeracy which had been incorporated into the lesson, and that there would also be adequate use of ICT...the checklist for the perfect lesson went on and on and on. I had to painstakingly follow this checklist six times. *Six.* Not to mention that the books had to be absolutely perfect.

The difference was, at Panaculty Academy I would have been beaten with a stick to do this and nothing was ever good enough for them. Here, as a supply teacher I didn't even have to do this, but I did it out of respect and loyalty to the school which had saved me. Yet this is a routine which is practiced by every teacher in the UK on a regular basis. The demands are simply way too high. They often result in a nine or ten hour work day at school, and then usually between four to six hours into the evening of marking and meticulous lesson preparation. If my maths is correct this could total a sixteen hour work day of which only half is actually paid for. Certainly in many countries, teachers from the UK are regarded as the best trained and most resilient in the world; however in England the unbearable pressure on staff is absolutely not sustainable.

Exhausted, I decided to try and grab a few hours of sleep. I would have a shot of wine for breakfast in the morning, to calm my nerves.

Thursday, 3rd March 2016
Newton Aycliffe, County Durham, England

The sound of the alarm was extremely unwelcome. I would have preferred to sellotape my eyeballs to a pigeon than experience this diabolical racket. Today was the day. They were coming. I imagined the inspectors waking up in the morning after a wonderful night's sleep, and being served a delicious variety of dishes for breakfast in their stately homes, perhaps smoked salmon and poached egg on English muffins. None of that for me. As good as it sounded, wine would do.

On the way to school, I blasted heavy rock music. I arrived at school wide awake, pumped up and ready to face these judgemental and out of touch callous individuals.
The atmosphere in the staffroom was very sombre. Like a funeral. There could almost have been a church organ solemnly playing in the background. The head teacher's words washed over me like an overplayed chart hit and the staff headed off to their classrooms.

They came, or rather; a female inspector came, into my second lesson, which was Year 8 Geography. A class of 36 boys who were very lively, yet I had grown to really love them. In this class there were Niall and Brian, who were lazy with their homework and presentation, yet insanely clever. They had written an amazing piece about flooding in Bangladesh which was very creatively based on Martin Luther King's speech. I had framed it and put it on the wall it was that good. There was also Adam Taunton, whose handwriting was almost illegible, yet his hand was always up and he could answer almost any question he was ever asked. What I found wonderful about this group of boys was that despite their low level of literacy and their intense dislike of English, they really seemed to enjoy geography, for which they often had to learn many challenging key terms such as 'saturation'. They participated enthusiastically every lesson without fail. And I loved them for that.

In this particular lesson I had planned an interactive quiz which involved the students working in groups of four, and completing a task sheet which was challenging and progressed in terms of difficulty. The students were using the OS (Ordnance Survey) maps of the North East of England, and as they had always seen them in the classroom yet seldom had the opportunity to explore and exploit them, they were excited. Students in general always did get excited at something different and undiscovered, as is human nature. They quickly got on with the tasks outlined in groups, animatedly discussing four and six figure grid references, contour lines, whether there was deciduous or coniferous wood cover, and scale. Out of the corner of my eye, I saw the inspector make a note in her file. As she had entered the classroom I was sure that the temperature had dropped by about 20 degrees. Although I had greeted her warmly and smiled at her, she had not returned my gesture.

Suddenly the inspector got up and began prowling around the classroom to look at books. 'If she loves to stare at books so much, why doesn't she go and sit in a library,' I thought to myself. I couldn't wait for her to leave me and my lovely Year 8 class alone to enjoy Geography without this feeling of unease. I noticed then that the inspector was poring over Adam Taunton's book. The boy with the illegible handwriting. I really hoped that the inspector would ignore this, and notice just how well he had performed in the quiz, and how much progress he had made with his map skills. Other students loved to work with him as he was so knowledgeable. If he was on their team they would almost always win. I noticed the inspector was talking to Adam. 'Brilliant,' I thought. 'Adam will be telling her about how he enjoys our lessons, and what he's learned so far this term.'

The boys worked impeccably all lesson and I felt elated by the end. They folded the OS maps neatly (which is difficult even for adults!) and were able to answer all of my plenary questions, showing that they certainly knew their stuff when it came to map skills. In the Geography GCSE exam, there are three papers: physical geography, human geography, and map skills. Of the three, the map skills section is often where the students perform the worst. As the bell rang, the inspector swept out of the door, and three students hung back. I thought this was very absurd, as usually their hunger would be so overwhelming by break time and they would rush to be the first in the queue at the tuck shop. I couldn't help but notice the students looked a little disheartened.

"Don't worry! I'm sure you'll win next time we do an activity like this! You were all brilliant," I beamed. I was proud of them.

"No it's not that, miss. That woman who was sitting there...she said Adam's work was a disgrace," said Connor.

"Connor, she wouldn't say that. That's a serious allegation!" I exclaimed. I was secretly happy that the students seemed to dislike the inspector as much as I did, though unless Donald Trump is involved, fake news is not to be encouraged.

"No miss – she did," butted in Adam. His cheeks were flushed red. He was telling the truth. I could tell.

"Right – I will have to tell Mrs Fortune what has happened, and I imagine that she will want to speak with you. Will that be alright?" I asked. Adam nodded, and the three boys turned to leave the classroom.

"Adam – your work is not a disgrace. That woman doesn't know who you are. But we all do. Don't worry." Adam managed a smile and left.

I knew that I should have gone to the head teacher first, but I wanted to hear the inspector's side before I did so. I power walked a couple of laps around the school and found the woman standing on the edge of the playground, clipboard in hand.

"Good morning – I'm Miss Wansdo – Lilee." I extended my hand. The inspector just looked down at it as though it was contaminated with a highly contagious disease. "Yes, I gathered. I'm sure you want to know what I thought of your geography lesson," replied the inspector. As I had anticipated, she spoke with an obnoxiously posh 'Received Pronunciation' accent, similar to that of Louise Haughty, who had actively enjoyed contributing to my days of misery at Panaculty Academy.

"Well – the students certainly enjoyed your lesson, and it's clear that you have a nice working relationship with those students, rooted in mutual respect," began the inspector. My breath caught in my throat. What was this? Positive feedback from an Ofsted inspector?! I couldn't believe it!

"However, those books are a disgrace. The work and presentation is completely substandard. How can those students make any progress if they can't even read what they've written? Some of the dates and titles weren't underlined. Some hadn't even written the date. Some of the diagrams hadn't been coloured in. I think they should learn basic presentation skills before you teach them geography!" The inspector guffawed, a bizarre sound.

The red mist descended as anger flared inside me. The judgemental horrible witch. How dare she come in there and slate young people who she doesn't even know, and judge them from data on a computer and whether they've underlined the date and title? I could handle it if the inspector attacked me, but not my students. That was totally unfair. But the inspector wasn't finished.

"And as for you, you weren't using or encouraging proper English. All teachers must demonstrate a good use of English to the students. Imagine if you had a student who had English as an additional language. How on earth would they understand you?" she guffawed again. Right, that was it.

"We are in the North East. This is how people speak. It's how I speak, it's how 99% of our students speak. It's how everyone in the community speaks. If I was to speak unnaturally, they wouldn't respond to me," I protested. I wanted to shout. I really wanted to say, 'do your background research first before you come here!' But out of respect for my colleagues, I didn't. Though I wasn't finished yet either.

"And I want to say one thing to you. This school has saved me. Coming here has kept me in the teaching profession. I nearly killed myself before because I was so unhappy. The head teacher is wonderful. She's doing a wonderful job for these children and the community, which has just been left to rot by the Tories. People have nothing but a Tesco and a benefit system now. They don't eat properly, their heating and electricity go off because they can't afford to top it up, and sometimes the students' parents make poor choices and spend their money on booze instead of looking after their kids... We show them the love and care that some of them desperately need. And then people like you come in here, and think you can complain about their dates and titles not being underlined-"
I had to stop. I was too worked up, and trying so hard not to swear at this belligerent woman.

"I would like you to apologise to Adam before the end of the day. You really upset him. He's an amazing student." I also wanted to say, 'and he has an awful home life. But you wouldn't know about anything like that,' but I didn't.

The look on the inspector's face was unexpected, yet worse than I could have imagined. She smiled smugly, like a vulture who had found a delicious meal after searching far and wide, and simply made another note on her clipboard before turning away, signalling that the conversation was finished. She'd heard all she needed to know. I was adamant that she'd written 'psychopath. Get rid of her,' on her notepad. The bell rang. I had to find someone to cover my next lesson quick so that I could speak to the head teacher. This couldn't wait. Kirsten had to know who we were dealing with. These were not normal Ofsted inspectors, but mutants, evolved to be even more cruel than before.

Kirsten Fortune sat up bolt upright when she heard what I had to tell her. I told her every detail. As I had predicted, she was shocked. This behaviour, even for an Ofsted inspector, was not normal.
"Are you absolutely certain?" she asked. I nodded.
"Right – I'll have someone fetch Adam straight away. You get back to your lesson. And Lilee – thank you for your little speech praising the school. Though you've probably made her day now – being 'saved by the school' is not what they will want to hear, nor respect - now they'll think we're a soft touch!" Kirsten half

grimaced, half smiled. The rest of the day passed in a blur.

The end of the day was fast approaching, and all members of staff were once again summoned to the staffroom. Mrs Fortune's face was grim as she addressed us.

"The lead inspector is...obtuse, to say the least," said the head teacher with obvious displeasure. "They have decided that they would like to spend another day here, which has never happened in this school before. So I won't keep you. Get home and get some rest and strength, and be ready for tomorrow. Good luck to us all."

As the staff left, I noticed an unwelcome shift in the atmosphere which had previously been so strong and positive. It was a feeling that was unfortunately all too familiar. It was the feeling of a school's strength and solidarity being crushed, stamped on, and torn apart.

I blasted Linkin Park and roared along loudly as I drove home, ready to repeat the same laborious planning as the night before. I hoped that something positive would happen, and that this school would not become enveloped in the same stifling and depressing atmosphere as Panaculty Academy had been.

Sadly, it did. For the first time in the school's history, it was downgraded from '2 - Good' to '3 - Requires Improvement.'

Chapter 4 – My Greek wedding

Saturday 9th April 2016
Newcastle upon Tyne, England

I hadn't eaten a thing all week. I could only drink.
Although my heart felt warm at the effort people were
making to attend the wedding which had been pulled
together in a matter of weeks, I was sick with nerves.
Friends had come from all over the country, and even
from France and Norway. We had decided in the end to
take everyone's advice and get married as it would be
easier to move abroad afterwards. I wasn't worried
about marrying Daniel; we rarely even argued, and
enjoyed each other's company. Surely it was just the
next stage of the relationship, and was totally natural.
I couldn't understand why I felt so awful.

Arguments had erupted over the invitations. As we had
just weeks to put a wedding together, I had requested
that we kept the guest list at an absolute minimum,
which meant no extended family such as random
cousins you only see once in a blue moon.
Unfortunately, Daniel was one of eight children, most of
whom had families of their own already, and so the
number of immediate family on his side stood at almost
30 people. However, Daniel's mum Maureen insisted
that all of the aunts, uncles, and cousins were to be
invited, to which I had replied, "you will have to help
pay for it then!"

The eventual guest list came to approximately 100 people, which was much more than I had wanted. I really didn't want to have to think about what the varied requirements and needs for all those people on the day would be. I just wanted to get hitched, have a bit of a party and be done with it. It was so much stress just for one day after all. There were already people whinging about who they would and wouldn't sit next to, people inventing new dietary requirements which I was sure they hadn't had before, and countless people asking for information which they could easily find out themselves, and I would direct them instantly to Google maps and the national rail website.

In the end Daniel's father had come to the rescue, and one of his clients (Daniel's father was a well-known and respected solicitor in the north east) had agreed to host the wedding reception in his Greek restaurant at a very generous discounted price. I knew that the food was gorgeous, so accepted the proposition without complaint. Daniel's brother and his band had agreed to play for free, and my friend's sister was a photographer, who had kindly agreed to do the photos at a generous discount. My mum had maxed out her credit card in order to buy the dress, a beautiful lace La Sposa one. The process of wedding dress shopping on a Saturday followed by a quick coffee and cake date had hugely improved the bond between mother and daughter, which had been somewhat frayed in the past.

Neither of us had made much headway in an attempt to repair the damage to our relationship before now. There had of course been previous attempts; mum had decorated a spare room for me in her cottage which had cost a lot of money, even though I hadn't lived with her since the divorce. Whenever I had made the long journey to the middle of rural Northumberland to visit her, we would always end up arguing fiercely about my father. Mum would always bring up the subject when I didn't want to talk about it, and then she would explode at my seemingly passive attitude. Consequently I no longer had any interest in travelling all the way there to partake in a warring confrontation that even parliament would have been envious of, preferring a much needed weekend of peace or drinks with friends.

Fortunately, the situation was becoming much better. Mum had a new job that she loved, still working as a nurse but on the community instead of being stuck in a hospital with health care assistants with a chip on their shoulder, and doctors who treated anyone below them like a used bed pan. She had also found herself a boyfriend, in the form of the next door neighbour, Stuart. He had attracted her by anonymously leaving boxes of eggs on her doorstep, so he was nicknamed by my brother and me as 'Humpty Dumpty', or 'Egg man'. He ran a gardening business and to our knowledge, there wasn't anything bad about him, just that he was a bit on the older side. He had arranged a minibus to transport people from the registry office to the Greek restaurant for the reception, which was his contribution to the wedding.

The thought suddenly struck me, that it was the morning of my wedding. My insides squirmed. My friend from Norway, Ingvild, was staying with me, and it was so nice to have her there. The make-up artist and hairdresser were coming at 10 o' clock, and there was still no sign of my four bridesmaids. Lou was coming from Doncaster, Izzy and Alissa from London, and Sally from the other side of Newcastle. I hoped they would all get along. They had all already met at the hen do in Manchester a couple of months earlier which had been an unforgettable night. Izzy had organised the whole thing; a cocktail making lesson at Revolution, and then a meal, followed by a male stripper cabaret performance which was absolutely hilarious. Everyone had laughed so hard their insides could have fallen out. At the time it had all been so exciting, the 'wow, I'm getting married!' kind of feeling. Yet now it felt terrifying.

Once everyone arrived, there was no time for a proper catch up like what normally happened when I met up with my friends who lived far away. The atmosphere was awkward and stiff, as everyone was sitting awkwardly on the sofa watching each person have their makeup done one at a time. Izzy handed me a glass of Prosecco. I felt so sick I threw it straight back up. No-one ever tells you how stressful a wedding can be, and there is no advance warning whatsoever! The wedding car arrived early, sending me into a massive panic. My brother and mum were late. I knew that mum was notorious for her lateness, but today of all days!?

I was beginning to worry that something had happened when they finally arrived at the house, mum flapping and panicking, making me even more on edge. My brother stood quietly behind mum, muttering under his breath about how the streets of Gateshead all looked the same, and was like a 'bloody druggie rabbit warren.' I ushered him quickly into the waiting car outside, feeling self-conscious that my fake tan was too orange, and that my dress didn't come in enough at the waist, hanging off my boobs and making me look chunkier than I already was. I had fallen in love with the size 12 sample dress in the shop, and it had fitted perfectly, somehow giving me a perfect hourglass figure. Sadly the shop owner had insisted that she would order a size 14 and that we could have it taken in and the fit would be better. It wasn't at all. The seamstress was so busy she did not have the care to listen to me, and so now my poor mum had spent a ghastly amount of money she didn't have on a dress that didn't fit me properly. Still, at least it wasn't too small! That would probably be much worse if I couldn't get into my dress on the day of the wedding. I prayed it was something that people joked about but never actually happened, though for some unlucky people, I supposed it did.

The car journey with my brother took no time at all. I would have liked to have stayed in there longer. The time passed so fast it was almost like we had flown there in a fighter jet. The car was beautiful, a white jaguar with huge shiny alloy wheels and a middle aged chauffeur dressed like they were in war time films. He was very friendly and very Geordie, and as soon as we got into the car he commented "eeeee! You look like a pair of film stars yous do like!" I made a mental note to thank him profusely for how much he helped to calm my nerves once I had got married.

As the car inched into the registry office car park, which was the only place we could get married where we both wouldn't burst into flames, according to Daniel, I could see my cousins, swaggering around with cans of cider. They had at least put on trousers for the occasion, though their usual hoodies were on, with the hoods up over a basketball cap. I wondered if they ever washed them. I imagined when, or if ever, they removed them, they would peel slowly and painfully from the dried sweat like a stuck plaster to skin. As the car pulled up outside, my brother began to speak. Bert was a man of few words, and I was wondering how he was going to manage with all of the small talk he would inevitably have to deal with from all the wedding guests.
"I'll go and check if they're ready for us."
I was alone in the car for only two minutes, when Izzy came up to the window. I opened the door and motioned for her to get in.
"Are you still alright to do that reading?" I mentioned.
"It doesn't matter if not." I knew from the immediate pained reaction on my friend's face that she had

forgotten all about it.

"Oh man, shit Lilee, I totally forgot! I'll get it on my phone quickly now!"
"Honestly don't worry about it, it's just words Izzy! Just having you here is the most important thing!"
Izzy wouldn't leave it. She rushed away to prepare herself, leaving me alone in the car again, of which I was glad so I had a few minutes to be alone with my thoughts. I began to daydream, picturing myself walking into the ceremony and how Daniel would look, all groomed and smart in a suit instead of his Nissan uniform. Would he be smiling or serious? Would the atmosphere be tense or relaxed? It was impossible to tell. I watched the guests filing into the venue, all dressed in their best, and I was once again humbled at how much effort everyone had gone to in order to attend. The only person who didn't look happy was Daniel's mum. I wasn't even sure if I had ever seen her smile. Her forehead was a graveyard of wrinkles; no crow's feet. That surely stood for something.

Suddenly a tap on the window distracted me from watching the guests clambering up the stairs to the registry office, and fretting about how I was now probably going to have to see a lot more of Daniel's mum. I looked up and was shocked at who I saw. It was Jeremy, my father.

The ceremony was short and very sweet and it passed quickly and smoothly within an hour. A couple of people cried, though neither Daniel nor I did. He was smiling and calm, which helped me immensely. He later told me that he had had a couple of whiskeys beforehand. We left the venue holding hands and smiling, albeit no confetti as it had been banned by the registry office. In the car, Daniel squeezed my hand and grinned. "Well we did it then, didn't we? No-one ran in screaming 'I object!'" We giggled. That was surely yet another thing that must be a worry for some people on their wedding day.

Throughout the entire wedding reception I was a bag of nerves. Although the staff really outdid themselves with all of our favourite Greek food; Halloumi cheese, beef Stifado, Souvlaki, Moussaka, and pulled pork Gyros, I couldn't eat a single morsel, although I would have loved to. I was sitting opposite Daniel's mum who looked like she was celebrating a funeral rather than a wedding, dressed in a black suit to symbolise the respectful mourning of the departed. She did not smile once, but glared at me vengefully across the table, saying nothing. She didn't have to say anything.

Deterred, I occupied myself by looking around at our guests to make sure they were having a good time, and to my dismay, saw three people on their phones. "Daniel, please go and see what the matter is. There are people sitting on their phones not talking to anyone. I knew it was going to be a nightmare with so many people not knowing each other!" Daniel was unfazed by this.

"Babes, chill! Everything's fine. We're celebrating! Let's have a drink! What do you want?" I knew that it wasn't sensible to drink without eating, but I just couldn't eat. "Wine, and lots of it!" I replied.
"That's my wife!" laughed Daniel, kissing me on the cheek.

Once the meal was over with and I could go and mingle with people that I actually liked, I began to relax a bit. The only downside was that I could only spend a maximum of five minutes with each person, many of whom I had not seen for absolutely ages, before someone would be tapping me on the shoulder and I would have to abruptly end the conversation that I had really wanted to continue. The most frequent offenders were people like Stuart, mum's boyfriend, who would pop up out of nowhere like a jack in the box. As the night went on, and everyone became merrier and merrier, the music got wilder and wilder. Once the band had finished, a playlist had been set up with an iPod dock which was now being hijacked by people with an extreme variety of musical tastes. Heavy death metal rock one minute, grime and R&B the next, followed by happy hard-core or trance. This caused some people to start complaining to us, and we were thankfully now drunk and confident enough to say "go and sort it yourselves."

The night passed in a flash, and ended with us both stepping out into the Bigg Market in Newcastle city centre on a Saturday night, to meet a resonating cheer that could easily have rivalled that of a Newcastle United football match at St James' Park. On a Saturday night, revellers swarmed the streets to spend their hard earned money in Newcastle's famous bars and clubs, and at this time, two in the morning, the party for everyone was in full swing. It was unforgettable.

Wednesday 8th June 2016
Newton Aycliffe, County Durham, England

Three months later and there were just six weeks left until the end of term, and Daniel and I would be ready to leave for Sri Lanka. The downgrade from 'good' to 'requires improvement' by Ofsted had, like an earthquake, caused ructions and repercussions not just in the school, but throughout the entire community. The reputation of the school and indeed the head teacher was ruined. The parent governors were angry. They wanted to see the changes which Ofsted had insisted on happen fast. The healthy climate had vanished. Instead of feeling like a new plant growing happily in a pot of soil, I felt like a sack of cement had been thrown on me. The meetings after school were much more frequent, and went on for much longer than they had done previously. The morale of staff was at an all-time low. Data tracking and pupil progress had gone into overdrive. The students also reacted negatively to such changes.

"I never used to get such shocking marks with Miss Collins. I only ever did the foundation paper. You don't know nothing about me miss!"

Beth Randall was in full kick off mode. She and her friend Georgina had not been so difficult until now. Unfortunately due to the new obsession with data and progress tracking generated by Ofsted, Beth's literacy SAT result from Year 5 had been a level 4a. That was five years ago, and she was now in Year 10. Therefore as the data 'flight path' predicted, she should be capable of achieving a B at GCSE. These systems didn't take into account what happened halfway through – puberty! And God knows what else. Despite her indignant protests, senior management had decided that she would be entered for the higher tier. Beth was not at all happy about this.

"Come on Beth, you can do it! You've always been good at Geography. Particularly coastal processes, which a lot of other people find difficult," I coaxed in the most encouraging tone I could muster. Unfortunately, it was to no avail. In protest, Beth tore the higher tier GCSE practice question booklet in half and threw it on the floor, sticking her middle finger up at me. The other students who had up until now been settled and working well, shrieked and giggled in shock. The lesson was quickly about to become as much entertainment for them as Saturday night television. I knew not to rise to it, and to remain calm and collected, as thin as my patience for such insolence was.

"Pick that up now Beth. You can copy the whole thing out again at break time. It's not fair to expect the photocopy lady, or anyone else for that matter, to do it again for you. "

I didn't expect what came next.

"You effing what miss?! This is *your* fault anyway! I told you I'm not doing higher. And you're trying to make me do it now against my will. That's forced child labour that is. Me mam'll kick your head in when I tell her," Beth Randall's screeching at 10,000 decibels pierced my eardrums like spears.

"Get out of my class, Beth. I'm not having this. This is a GCSE class. If you're going to carry on like a child, primary school is back down the road. Go to the library, and copy up the work you decided would be a good idea to rip up."

"Make me. Come on then! I'd have you in a fight me like!" Beth sprang out of her seat, her greasy black hair swinging with energy, eyes narrowed.

I opened the door. "Out," I said. It should have been a simple room removal, situation dealt with. However Beth had other ideas. She lunged forward, shoved me against the board and slapped me hard in the face before storming out and away down the corridor. I felt dizzy, and tears began to sting my eyes as I tried to quickly come to terms with what had happened. I had to get out of there quick before anyone saw. I couldn't believe it was all happening all over again. I wondered what attitude senior management, who up until the visit from Ofsted had been so supportive, would take.

I barricaded myself in the humanities department storage room, sat on a stool and sobbed and sobbed. Why oh why, had I decided to do this thankless job? Teaching certainly wasn't a career where I thought that I could be at risk of being attacked every day. Things had seemed so much better, but now here I was, back to where I was not so long ago. It had to be me that was the problem. I also began to wonder if this was in some way karma. Though I had been troublesome and mischievous at school, I had never been so obnoxious, let alone attacked a teacher. Within just half a year this had now happened to me twice, in two different schools.

I recalled Dr Pope, who had been my biology teacher when I was at school. He must have been newly qualified and fresh from university, and had affectionately written in my yearbook: 'The sight of water flying around my classroom will haunt me forever'. I smiled guiltily as I remembered my fearless fourteen year old self. During a lesson about osmosis, I had turned one of the taps in the science lab upside down, and then spun the tap round to full blast. Half of the class had been instantly drenched, and Dr Pope's expression of sheer devastation on his youthful face had stayed in my mind forever since. I had of course written a letter of apology to him, and my parents had punished me severely at home. Dr Pope had said on the day that I had left school that it was alright, and that he had long forgiven me and that he saw I had shown remorse. "We all make mistakes," he had smiled kindly. "As long as you take responsibility for them, you will continue to learn."

I hadn't seen any remorse from my students, who had committed much more serious crimes than giving the class a free shower, and it scared me how cold and emotionless they could be. What would they be like as adults?

Going to Sri Lanka was definitely the right decision, I decided right then and there. It was that moment, then, that I knew in my sinking heart that I would probably never set foot back in the UK to teach ever again. The only thing that could ever lure me back for a week or two was mum's cooking, and my wonderful friends.

The next six weeks passed in a blur as I reverted to the mechanical 'day in, day out' rhythm that I had used previously to survive at Panaculty Academy. Switching onto autopilot was the only way to get through. On my last day, which was also the last day of the academic year 2016, I had made certificates for all of the students in my Year 7 tutor group so that those who hadn't achieved a prize for achievement or progress still had some recognition. I thought that they would be happy to take home a certificate and some chocolate to show whoever they lived with at home, and end Year 7 on a positive note, no matter what.

I had gone to the printer shop especially the night before, and paid with my own money to create elaborate certificates printed on shiny gold paper. For Charity, she would receive a certificate for the most skilled debater, Helen for being the most approachable and caring member of the class, and Jayden, who had constantly been in trouble throughout the year, would receive a certificate praising his witty sense of humour. I felt sure that it might make him smile. As I awarded the certificates at the front of the class on my last day, Jayden simply crumpled his up, and threw it carelessly in the bin. The girls gasped, genuinely appalled at his reaction.

"Jayden, that's horrible!" said one of the girls.
"Apologise to miss!"

Jayden glanced up, and looked at me right in the eyes. "Good riddance. I'm glad you're fucking off," he said harshly, before walking out of the classroom. Instead of allowing his words to hurt me, as they would have done previously, I simply smiled. I was gleeful, delirious, that I was getting away from a place which harboured such horrors. I just knew that Sri Lanka would be different. Of course there had been some lovely children at Haggerty Academy too, but sadly there was just way too many who had no care or compassion in their hearts. I was done. I had had enough of trying to help those who didn't want my help. I had to put myself first, like everyone else seemed to.

"Have a nice life!" I said loosely, before grabbing my bag and bouncing out of the classroom that I would never set foot in again. I felt no sadness, only sympathy for my colleagues who couldn't get out, stuck at home with their families, having to come back and face this day in and day out. This was not going to be my life too. I knew it was about to change forever.

Monday 8th August 2016
London Heathrow Airport, England

"I'm really going to miss you. All these years we wasted...arguing and fighting..." mum sobbed. It was awful.

"We give them roots to grow, and wings to fly," beamed Daniel's dad. I was really glad that he was there. It made the goodbye much easier. My new school in Sri Lanka had booked the flight out from London Heathrow, eight hours drive away from Newcastle. Amazingly, Daniel's dad had agreed to drive us down early in the morning, which meant that we would be there in plenty of time before our twelve hour long flight at nine that evening. I was very familiar with Heathrow airport, having flown out of there many times, as unfortunately Newcastle airport only catered for hen and stag do destinations, such as Malaga, Ibiza, or Ayia Napa.

I was really grateful for how upbeat Daniel's dad was as we made the journey down there. It was a surreal experience, not knowing what we would face once we arrived, or whether we would even be happy, and considering how we would deal with missing everyone and having to start a whole new circle of friends. We arrived at Heathrow airport at just before two in the afternoon, which was seven hours before our flight was due to leave. We hit the airport bar in a big celebration of the new chapter that we were about to embark on, and perhaps also drowning our sorrows of all our loved ones that we were leaving behind. How we made it on to the plane, I would never know.

As we stepped onto the plane, although I really hated flying, I knew that it was the best decision I had ever made. Although maybe it wouldn't be for Daniel.

Chapter 5 – Hurry, Vagina monologues

Monday 22th August 2016
Kandy, Sri Lanka

We had decided to arrive in Sri Lanka early in order to get settled before school started on the 29th, and we had spent the first few days of our new life on the coast in Negombo, which had been very quiet. We had not realised that August was low season in the west and south of Sri Lanka, though the sun still shined with all of its formidable strength. Daniel had bought some 'factor 90 St. Ives' sun lotion from a shop across the road from the hotel, which turned out to be completely fake. He applied the cream all over his body and lay in the midday sun all afternoon, only to be left in agonising pain in the evening. For Daniel this was rather unexpected, as he usually had the right skin for tanning and would quickly go cinnamon brown in the sun. He even used to use sunbeds regularly when he was younger to look tanned for girls. However, the strength of the sun here in the tropics was far superior to that of continental and Mediterranean Europe, yet neither of us had realised that it would be to this extent. Daniel had no choice but to spend two full days in the comfort of the air conditioned hotel room, while his skin blistered and shed like one of Sri Lanka's many snakes.

The school had arranged for Vijaya, the head of Maths to pick us up from the train station in Kandy with his wife, and he had taken us to an apartment which would be our new home. It was larger than the crummy flat we had rented back in Gateshead, with a tiled floor and small front garden. There was a state of the art washing machine, the American style one like in the films, where you bung your clothes easily in through the top lid, instead of having to push and shove them all in through a small side door as many typical washing machines are in the UK.

The cooking facilities were a little limited, just a dual gas stove, a fridge, and a table, with no pans or oven. As it was the school that would pay the first three months of rent, I did not feel in a position to complain, although it later emerged there was no ceiling fan, let alone air conditioning, and the shower had less pressure than trickling glacial melt water. In high insight, we should maybe have asked that these issues be fixed before we moved in or ask the school to find us a different place, but I did not want to start on a bad note.

"You can call me Anagi if it's easier for you," the landlady had said grandly before ambling back up the small road to her house. When I repeated her name five minutes later, I was cut off by Vijaya's cold and unsmiling wife. She could have been very pretty if she learned how to smile.

"Not Anagi. *Mrs* Nugawela," she said, emphasising the 'Mrs' heavily.

The landlords themselves, Mr and Mrs Nugawela, were principals of the Waraka International School, and a sweet elderly couple, in their late seventies! I couldn't believe they were even still teaching, let alone be active principals of a school! Mrs Nugawela dressed elegantly in a sari every day without fail and would come down to the house every evening to check that we were alright. At first, we remarked that this was very sweet and thoughtful, until we realised that not one move that we made would ever go unnoticed. It began to annoy us and in fact slightly scare us, when Mrs Nugawela would phone us on a Friday night at 8pm and ask where we were, and why we were not at home. She would also decide when to collect our washing in, or come in to 'clean' when she felt like it. Some may have appreciated this help and gesture of goodwill, but for a young couple who had been used to complete privacy in the UK this was downright intrusive. I decided to speak to

Mrs Nugawela about this, as diplomatically as possible. The school was paying the rent, after all.

"Mrs Nugawela, we really appreciate how you're thinking of us and trying to help us, but we really would prefer it if you could respect our privacy," I began. "I know that we are here, in your country, and things might be different here, but usually landlords have no right to come onto, or into the property without giving at least 24 hours' notice. They also cannot phone you unless it is an emergency-" I stopped then, for Mrs Nugawela was waving her hand gently.

"Oh, yes I know it's different there, dear. My daughter was in the UK you know for university, in Cambridge. We went up to the Lake District for a weekend. We really loved it, especially the fish and chips! I tried to get on a bus there once, the way we do here, and I was told to get down! And my husband tried to burn rubbish on the street in Cambridge outside my daughter's house... even though we told him not to. He can't do that there!" Both Mrs Nugawela and I were then laughing hard, she was holding her sides from laughter; I had my hands over my mouth laughing in disbelief.
"I'm sorry if we disturbed you, dear. Please come to our prize giving event on Friday – it will be most motivating for the students in our school. I'll give you a sari to wear."

She had been so kind and easy to talk to, and we had shared a lovely moment of laughter together. Despite

re-reading my school contract and noting that one of
the clauses specifically outlined that I was under
absolutely no circumstances to offer service to another
school or institution, whether paid or unpaid, we
decided that we would come to the prize giving event to
be polite. We would not let Mr and Mrs Nugawela
down.

Saturday 27th August 2016
Kandy, Sri Lanka

I had had a huge argument with Daniel the night before
the prize giving ceremony. He had drunk too much, and
passed out on the bed, snoring with such force the
windows quivered in their wooden frames. His breath
was so rancid it almost made me retch. I tried countless
times to wake him yet it was impossible, and I ended up
sleeping on the sofa in frustration, catching barely an
hour's sleep. The event was due to begin at eight
o'clock in the morning, and it was almost six already.
Fumbling amongst the six yards of sari material, I found
the blouse which I had picked up a few days ago from
the tailor, a lovely lady called Mangala.

"I hope she doesn't *mangle* the material," Daniel had
said. It wasn't mangled, though it was so tight it was
extremely difficult to wiggle my shoulders or even pick
up anything. My boobs were so compressed they ached,
and in a moment of horror, I began to fret at what little
I could possibly do if they itched. In the cooler morning
it was manageable, though I worried at what on earth

would happen in the searing heat and humidity of midday. Visions of being interrogated in a hospital bed as surgeons attempted to peel the material which had fused together with my sweat and stuck rigidly to my upper torso, danced in my mind. In Sri Lanka teachers in the government schools were expected to wear these every day. I could barely stand in the darned thing, let alone teach!

Putting on the underskirt as the tailor had instructed me to, I realised Daniel would have to help me. This was not a one woman job. I had watched countless YouTube videos the night before which had only frustrated me further as they had made it all look so easy, smiling and whirling around in their beautiful saris patronisingly. Thankfully, despite our argument the previous night Daniel woke quickly and helped, pinning the piece of material called the *fall* to the underskirt around my waist, to the blouse on my chest and over the top of my left shoulder, before wrapping the remainder of the material around my midriff and pinning securely, or so we hoped. As we jumped into the *three wheeler,* or *tuk tuk,* or rather, I inched into the three wheeler with a variety of robotic-like stances, terrified that this highly uncomfortable wad of material would plummet to the floor at any second and I would forever be known as the *suddi (*white woman) who had tried and catastrophically failed to wear a sari. "Have you got a brooch or any jewellery to go with it?" the driver Gavesh had asked. "He's got to be having a laugh! This is more than enough effort for one day!" I said hotly. Daniel smiled. He hadn't said much that morning except that he was suffering from a nasty hangover and that hopefully this prize giving event, whatever it was, would be over quite quickly.

Gavesh's number had been passed on to me by the school, and he had come highly recommended as a friendly, safe and pleasant driver.

It was thanks to Gavesh that I very quickly learned the meaning of the very commonly used 'hari hari!' in Sinhala, one of the main languages in Sri Lanka. There was Tamil too, which was much more spoken in the north and east of the island. As Gavesh pulled over at a small shop so we could buy some water, he leaned over in conversation with a passer-by standing next to the shop, waving his arm casually saying 'hari hari hari.'

I mistook his words for 'hurry hurry hurry!' and had responded irritably, as one thing I really couldn't stand was being rushed.

"Chill out Gavesh! Give me a minute!"

Gavesh had shrugged, nonplussed, before saying 'Hari, hari' again.

"I'm waiting for my change, Gavesh! I can't go any faster man!"

"Hari, hari."

My irritability was beginning to turn to fury, and as I returned to the Tuk Tuk I asked Gavesh again, exasperated.

"Why are you so angry?"

"No, Madam, not angry at all!"

"Then why do you keep telling me to hurry up?"

"Hurry...up? Hurry...aaaaah!" Gavesh burst out into jolly laughter.

"Hari Hari is not angry. It means like...ok."

"Hari means ok?"

"Yes Madam."

When we arrived at the venue, people stared at us as though we were an endangered species in a zoo, as we stood, dressed in our best, ready to enter the prize giving ceremony. No-one made any effort to speak to us. They just stared. We were escorted into the auditorium by a student, dressed impeccably in a white school uniform with a maroon blazer. We saw Mr and Mrs Nugawela sitting grandly on the stage in throne-like chairs, and so we waved and smiled enthusiastically at them. Either they did not see us, or chose not to acknowledge us. It was already beginning to get extremely hot, and the fans spinning feebly from the ceiling weren't even powerful enough to dissuade a mosquito from its flight path.

We waited for almost an hour before anything happened, reading the pamphlet outlining the order of service which was the only thing we could do to slightly relieve us of such excruciating boredom. We noted that most of the teachers did not even have a degree in their subject, let alone a masters or PGCE qualification, with many having only 'A level' in brackets next to their name under the section with the heading 'staffs.'

Despite being an 'international school' which followed the British International curriculum in English medium, the language in the pamphlet was so full of mistakes half of it did not make sense. I had read online about the dangers of some schools which were setting up for profit, calling themselves international schools, but usually they were run by already wealthy businessmen who wanted to swallow up even more money. Not too dissimilar to academies in the UK, to be honest.

Suddenly the sound of someone blowing through a conch shell with all their might pierced the air, followed by some rampant Kandyan drumming. We saw a group of well-dressed and highly official looking people, including Mr and Mrs Nugawela standing in front of a large golden ornament, adorned with round trays at numerous different levels, complete with a rooster on the top. It had been elaborately decorated with jasmine flowers, which cascaded elegantly down its long and slender neck. It was almost like a wedding cake equivalent for an antiques collector. We realised that this magnificent object was in fact a large oil lamp once we realised that the Nugawela's were holding string pieces, the flame dancing as they lowered the string to rest on the edge of one of the rounded trays of the oil lamp. Their facial expressions were so serious it was slightly unsettling, and we almost forgot entirely that this was an event for a school!

The prize giving ceremony went on for much longer than we had anticipated. The honoured guests drawled through their mundane speeches, the temperature in the auditorium rose insurmountably, and the supply of prizes which lay on the table on the stage slowly began to dwindle. Students who had walked onto the stage to be awarded their prizes knelt at the feet of Mrs Nugawela, and bowed their head to the ground, showing their utmost admiration and worship for their headmistress for all to see. I nudged Daniel in surprise when I realised once again just how different things were going to be here.

"That would *never* happen in the UK! The only time I've ever seen a student on the floor in that position before is when they've been kneed where it hurts!" Daniel chuckled, shaking his head. Eventually, and thankfully, the ceremony came to a long awaited end, and we were bundled into a van with some of the other teachers, which we were told would take us to a fancy hotel close to Kandy Lake, where we would enjoy a buffet lunch. "I hope it's a lovely rice and curry buffet, in those gorgeous clay pots! And there had better be beer. I'm absolutely clamming for a drink!" I whispered excitedly to Daniel.

Neither of us expected what happened when we arrived. Quickly, Daniel was ushered off into the section of the restaurant where there was a bar, and I was told to stay with the rest of the sari wearing women. We had not been prepared for this separation at all, and we did not welcome it either. When I asked Mrs Nugawela if I should order a bottle of red wine for our table, I was initially ignored, and when I asked again, I was met with an awkward smile, yet no verbal response. I glanced over to the other side of the restaurant, where all the men, including Daniel, were laughing merrily and drinking whiskey. I thought whether to ask if I could join Daniel, or just get up and go there myself, but something about this separation seemed particularly brutal, and I felt that I should not question it. It felt as though I was in a theme park, queuing for a rollercoaster ride, only to be told that I was not allowed to board as I was too short, and everyone else could go. Another disappointment was that the food was not a traditional and lovingly cooked rice and curry buffet, but instead they had tried, and failed tremendously, to prepare European food. Pasta with ketchup. Nothing else. Just ketchup. At this point, I decided to send Daniel a text message, praying that he would think to check his phone.

"Let's get out of here quick. Say you have diarrhea. No-one ever asks questions if you say that!" Sadly, Daniel didn't check his phone. He didn't need to, he was having a great time! I decided to attempt to make some small talk with the elderly lady seated opposite me. Her hair was pinned tightly in a severe bun, her face sallow and expressionless, though I had to remark that she had grown old gracefully.

"It's great for the school that you both came. I don't think we've ever had white people at our prize giving before. Parents will talk, and hopefully our admissions will begin to go up instead of down soon!"

Bile rose in my throat as it dawned on me that we had been invited there just because of how we looked, and used. Neither Mr nor Mrs Nugawela had even bothered to look at us, let alone speak to us, until I had been reunited with Daniel and we were about to leave. I had taken my phone out of my bag to check the time, and my background photograph of my friends Izzy, Alissa and I on my wedding day flashed across the screen, which Mrs Nugawela saw.
"You are friends with black people!? You are crazy!"
The idiocy of her words hit my face at full pelt, leaving my mouth hanging open, aghast. If this comment had been made by a drunken fool in a pub, I would kind of been prepared for it. But this lady was supposed to be the head teacher of a school!

I knew already that Mrs Nugawela was not used to being spoken to or challenged like this at all, and just a couple of hours ago she had had students worshipping her at her feet. But I could not hide the anger and dislike in my voice as I defended my friends against such an ugly and unjust comment.
"They're two of my best friends. They were my bridesmaids, on my wedding day. What does it matter whether they are black or white? Have you not heard that famous Michael Jackson song?"
Mrs Nugawela drew in her breath and pulled a very

forced smile before walking away. Daniel smirked.

"You know she's from a completely different era? In her day it was unheard of for whites to even talk to blacks. It must be alien for her."

"You can't make excuses for her! She can't have this archaic and downright awful mentality if she is a school principal!"

It was then, already, that I realised Mrs Nugawela could never be someone with whom I could share a close bond or friendship. Both my generation, and culture, were too different from everything she had ever been taught and known. Alien, as Daniel had said. We agreed that we would stay out of her way, and try to keep her at as much of a distance from our daily lives as possible. Unfortunately we would soon learn that she was certainly not on the same wavelength as us, and very much intended to become involved in our lives.

Monday 29th August 2016
Kandy, Sri Lanka

The morning dawned bright and clear, as the sun brought with it a new beginning. I had no idea what to wear, no idea what to expect from my new colleagues or students. I already had a preconceived idea that the students would be silent and respectful, and the teachers very strict. Having had a real baptism of fire in terms of teaching practice, I was ready to step into a completely new environment.

I had already visited the school the previous week with Daniel to meet with the head teacher before the academic term began. Sat in a large comfortable chair, surrounded by old fashioned and very elegant wooden panelling, with his name hand stencilled and painted above his door, Mr. Ranawana glanced up at us and motioned for us to enter his office. A head teacher's lair was rarely a pleasant place for a teacher, or for students, and you were almost always summoned there for doing something wrong, as to be quite honest head teachers usually do not have the time for anything else. I remembered my old school, where we had only ever seen the head teacher if there was something that would require his handshake, or for his photo to be taken for the local newspaper and he would be there within seconds. His presence in the school corridor was rarer than the chances of caviar being served at McDonalds. I wondered how much presence Mr. Ranawana would have in the school.

The first thing that I noticed was that Mr. Ranawana had to be around the same age as Mr and Mrs Nugawela, easily in his seventies. I wondered if they were friends, meeting up at weekends for dinner and drinks, grumbling about mediocre topics like politics and the crossword in the Sunday times, and 'how it was all so much better in those days' as people belonging to that generation usually did. When he began to speak, briefly summarising the running of the school day, I warmed to him immediately. He spoke with humour and honesty, and I silently appreciated his down to earth approach as the conversation drifted away from work, and he told us how ridiculous it was that he and his wife had wished to visit Thailand, yet for some unknown reason, their application for a tourist visa had been rejected. "Useless! Bloody disgusting!" he had uttered in his wonderfully Sri Lankan accent, which was very pleasing to the ears.

"How do we go about getting bank accounts? If we need proof of address, we're going to have to wait for ages until we get a utility bill with our names accompanying the address," I queried. We were met with a knowing smile as the head teacher lifted the telephone receiver on his desk.
"You can do anything here, if you know the right people. Or have money," he said bluntly, the knowing smile still on his face as he waited for whoever he was calling to answer the phone.
"Ahh, hello. It's Mr. Ranawana here calling from Thambili International. Yes. I have a new expat teacher here and she needs to open a bank account with you. Can I send her? Ok, right, right." He placed the telephone back on the desk, and wobbled his head in the way that appeared to be customary here, and although we had already seen it a fair few times we still weren't entirely sure what it meant. We warmly bade goodbye and made to leave, when Mr. Ranawana suddenly looked up and addressed Daniel.
"And you, what are your plans while you're here?"

Daniel shrugged and joked, "Well for now, I'm just enjoying being a kept man!"
"He worked as a chef before in England, then in a factory. He also did the TEFL online certificate to teach English before we left. I'm sure he'll find something once we get settled in," I gabbled. Mr. Ranawana said nothing, but stared back at us with a look of bemusement on his face, before saying that he would see me on Monday at 7.30 in the morning, and that we were to call him if there was anything we needed.

Daniel would have to find work soon, and we had spoken about this before we left, with me often pestering him to get looking and applying for anything we could find online. He hadn't much success in terms of finding employment, and we had been warned back when I had had the interview that as Sri Lanka was a country where jobs were very hard to come by, it was very difficult indeed for a foreigner to be hired outside of the educational field. In order to get work, you had to be able to prove to the immigration authorities that you were more qualified than a Sri Lankan to do the job. In my case I was able to, however Daniel didn't even have A levels, just a smattering of C – D grade GCSE's. I was already beginning to feel very dubious, yet he felt confident that as a native speaker of English he would almost certainly be hired.
"That's how it is in Thailand, my brother told me," he said, smiling. "It won't take long to find something, you'll see."

I arrived half an hour early on Monday 29th August at seven in the morning. In the UK I wouldn't even have been out of bed at that time, even on a school day. I hadn't slept that well the night before, possibly due to the cacophony of howling street dogs who had kindly decided to convene at the bottom of our road to stage their three a.m. scheduled performance. In spite of this I felt wide awake as I clambered up the smooth cement stairs into the staffroom, where we were to have the first staff meeting of the school year. I was warmly greeted by three elderly Sri Lankan gentlemen, who introduced themselves as Mr. Tishan, Mr. Abeywardana, and Mr. Wijesinghe; the art, business, and history teachers.

They spoke excitedly and proudly about their country, and asked eagerly where I had visited, and how I was finding the food. The first thought that struck me was how humble and sweet they were. The second thought was, *'what is it with Sri Lanka, and teachers who would have already been retired for at least ten years in Europe!?'* I had to admit that it was pretty impressive, though a part of me guiltily wondered how capable they would still be as teachers. *'Probably because the throw away culture of the west still isn't a thing here, which I came all this way to leave behind,'* I thought to myself. Of the three gentlemen, two spoke with very heavy accents, and their English was extremely hard to understand. Again, I realised with a pang of guilt that I did not speak their language, Sinhala, and their life

experience exceeded my own at least three times over.
I felt ashamed of myself for instantly finding their faults,
rather than praising them for their friendliness and
welcoming nature, which was becoming more and more
rare to find in many workplaces, and I quickly realised
that I would have to change, evolve from the callous
and cold being that I had been moulded into.

"It's always so nice to see a new face!" exclaimed a
smiling lady in a colourful fuchsia hijab. Her smile had
such strength it reached her eyes, which were warm
and approachable. She introduced herself as Faiqa, one
of the English teachers.
"Come, you must meet your department. Ahh Malcolm!
How was the holiday?" she addressed a man who had
just walked into the staffroom, who was overweight
and had a very ruddy complexion.

"It was great, thank you. Had a nice time visiting my
family. Mum was happy to see me." As Malcolm spoke, I
noticed two things. One, that he had a very strong
Glaswegian accent. Two, that he stuck his tongue out
and licked his lips before he began each sentence, like a
hugely swollen lizard. I wondered why that was. He
broke into a wide smile once he saw me and shook my
hand firmly. "Hiya! You must be Lilee. Welcome to the
department. When I received your application form and
saw that you were from Geordie land, I didn't need to
read much further! Why didn't you respond to my e-
mails? I sent you loads!"

I returned the smile before frowning slightly, puzzled.
"I didn't get any e-mails," I said slowly.

"I kept e-mailing the lady who I was in contact with
following my application, Ushmila I think her name
was? But she never replied, until about two weeks
before we were due to come here! We were getting
worried. I started to think the school had taken back
their decision!" I laughed.

"Ushmila? You mean 'Ushless.'" Said Malcolm,
beginning to laugh loudly. "That's what we all call her
here. *'Ushless', 'useless',* get it?"

I laughed nervously; worried in case I joined in the joke
and fell into an unknown trap, like Ushmila was
Malcolm's wife or something. Malcolm handed me
what I assumed was my new timetable.

"You've only got one lesson today. Year 8 German.
They're a nice bunch, but you've got two European kids
in there who are probably the worst behaved in the
school." He pulled a face. "Not the smoothest start, but
compared to what you've probably come from this will
be a piece of cake for you I'm sure." The bell rang
suddenly, barring the flood of questions that were on
the tip of my tongue. The teachers meandered
gracefully out of the staffroom towards assembly, some
clad in elegant saris, some in suits, some in dresses.

We took our seats on the stage in the auditorium,
where teachers were required to sit at the beginning of
each term, and watched as Mr Ranawana delivered his
welcome assembly. It was anything but welcoming.

"You are all..........yoooouuuseless. Your parents are equally............yoooouseless," bellowed the head teacher as he began to address the school at the beginning of the first term of the academic year 2016-17. He paused before each burst of 'useless', as if to ensure the maximum effect possible as he blasted the students for not pulling their weight in the exams. Malcolm nudged me and for that moment I hated him, as I was already trying not to split my sides from holding in my laughter. I had taken a liking to Mr Ranawana and I instantly respected him as a strong leader, owing to his clear 'no nonsense' attitude. It was, however, taking a while to become accustomed to the fact that his favourite word was 'useless'. It would never sound the same again after he had said it. I was soon to discover that the word 'useless' was one example of words that were very commonly used by many Sri Lankans but not as frequently by speakers of English from other countries. Instead of saying 'goodbye,' the phrase 'I'll go and come' was more commonplace, as well as affectionately referring to someone as 'this fellow.'

Back in the staffroom after the short and bizarre assembly, I studied my timetable that Malcolm had handed me earlier, and was amazed to see that I only had 18 lessons.

"I'm sorry you've got a bit more than everyone else. Normally it's between 14 -16 lessons per week, but Arjee has poached you for Geography as well... there wasn't really a lot we could do." I was even more shocked at Malcolm's apologetic tone. Was he being serious?!

"That's…amazing! I was doing 27 a week in the UK and it was way too much. I expected it would be a bit less here, like 22 maybe, but not 18! I'm absolutely fine with that, don't worry!" I smiled at Malcolm, which he returned as he leant forward and whispered, "don't go shouting around about that, or someone will take full advantage!"

The rest of the morning passed in a blur as I collected my books from the library, obtained library and computer accounts, and planned my lessons. Having basically no technology in the classrooms was going to be the biggest challenge. In all previous schools in the UK that I had worked in, each classroom had boasted a computer, iPad trolley, and an interactive whiteboard, complete with animated and colourful displays which stretched along every vein and artery of the school. I winced as I recalled the time at Panaculty Academy, where I had spent days labouring over a classroom display of the francophone world for the students. It was most possibly the best display I had ever created; and was complete with flags and colourful posters purchased from my own money, as well as QR codes which students could scan using their phones or iPads to access videos and quizzes about the French speaking world. All of my effort to enlighten the local community had been in vain however; within a fortnight half of the display had been torn down, and the other half was beautifully decorated with questionable male genitalia.

Here at Thambili International, there were no displays to be seen, neither in the classrooms nor in the corridors. Each classroom had a few metal tables and chairs and a whiteboard. That was it. I found it overwhelming that this was the most expensive and prestigious school outside of Colombo, where parents paid 100,000 rupees (approximately 500 pounds) per term to send their children here for the best possible education. There were no iPads or interactive whiteboards anywhere in the building, and the two computer labs were equipped with very old and extremely temperamental machines. It was no wonder really, as the IT technician had said with a cheeky grin: "Everything is illegally downloaded. You can buy the CDs with all of the Microsoft software for just a few rupees!" I would soon discover why there was so little ambition to roll out more technology at Thambili International; the local network was riddled with more viruses than a sexual health clinic in central Newcastle.

Despite the lack of technological facilities, the children were so prodigiously happy. As I entered the classroom to meet this Year 8 class for the first time, the metal chairs scraped and screeched on the concrete floor as the students stood up in silence.
"Good afternoon, ma'am," they choroused in unison.

The first thing that I noticed was how much more like children they looked. The girls were fresh faced, with no makeup caked all over their skin or hideous spider-like eyelash extensions. At Panaculty Academy an analysis of the wastepaper bin would usually show a count of more makeup wipes than paper. The boys looked smart too, their hair short and neat and no glimmer of greasy hair gel in sight. There were only twelve students; six boys and six girls. I was ever so slightly shell-shocked that they had stood up in silence when I had entered the room, and it was the first time in my three years of teaching that I had experienced this level of respect. It felt very alien.

A quick scan of the register scared me slightly. Some of the students had incredibly long names, or simply just too many of them. I would soon learn that it is very commonplace in Sri Lanka to place the family name both at the beginning and end of the endless train that is their name. After the first family name comes the caste, and this is then followed by the student's first and middle names, and however many the parents feel like adding after that.

This example shows a person with five names, though it is possible for one to have up to 14 names!

Weeraratne Mudiyanselage Bhanuka Dilantha Weeraratne

Family name   Caste   First names   Family name

The students were from a variety of different backgrounds. There was one boy who was half Swiss, half Sri Lankan, one who was half Welsh, half American, a girl who was half British, half Sri Lankan, two Muslim boys, two Buddhist boys and four Buddhist girls, and a Burgher. Burghers are not edible children, but are Sri Lankans who have European ancestry, and usually have surnames such as Fernando, de Silva, and Perera.

The first thing I endeavoured to do during the lesson was to learn their names as well as get an understanding of their current level in German. Having studied the language last year, I assumed that they would be familiar with the present tense. Their enthusiasm was infectious; and I soon had them playing imaginary tennis in pairs but using German phrases instead of a tennis ball.

"Ich gehe gern wandern."   *I like to go hiking.*
"Er geht gern wandern."   *He likes to go hiking.*

Their pronunciation was very good, and I told them so. I was met with innocent and genuine smiles and it was clear that these children liked to learn. I noticed that they already had a range of vocabulary that could probably far outweigh that of the Year 10 or 11 students at Panaculty Academy.

That night, Malcolm invited Daniel and I out for a drink at the Plabian bar, a pleasant place with lovely staff, though someone really needed to tell them to brighten the place up. It was so dark after 6pm your eyes began to hurt straining to locate your half full bottle of *Lion* beer amongst the empty ones. The three of us quickly lapsed into easy chatting and laughter, happily realising that we shared similarities such as instant openness, friendliness, and alarming generosity when it comes to whiskey. We were all beside ourselves with laughter at one of Malcolm's stories. Before beginning the post of the head of the languages department at Thambili international school, he had previously taught in Qatar and Saudi Arabia. Whilst he was in Qatar, he had taught the 14th daughter of the Qatari royal family, whose name was 'Mayassa'. As she was the Sheikh's daughter, she would be addressed as 'Sheikha.' Therefore her full name was; no word of a lie: 'Sheikha Mayassa'. Malcolm told this story again and again, and was met with the same reaction of glorious hysteria each time.

Suddenly, the heads of the Maths and Science departments showed up, stumbling around in the darkness like blind mice. They looked comical; one very large and rotund and the other pencil thin. Almost like the late comedians *Stan Laurel and Oliver Hardy*. It was only around 8pm, yet they were both absolutely blotto. I recognised the pencil thin man as Vijaya, the head of Maths, who had allegedly found our apartment for us, and was very close with our landlords, who we now called Mr and Mrs Judgemental (Nugawela). I did not recognise the much larger man.

"I'm noooooooot going out with you again sir!" roared Vijaya, wagging his finger in warning at the fat man, who was sitting lopsided on his bar stool, gazing at him vacantly in a drunken oblivion. The thin one began to rant at speed, as though he was rushing to create a bad opinion of his overweight colleague before anyone had actually had a chance to establish their own first impression of him. Malcolm, Daniel and I listened in amazement, six eyebrows skimming three hairlines, as the thin man proceeded to destroy his colleague's reputation in minutes, who was sitting right beside him! He told of how he started fights, how he was a lousy husband and father, and how he needed to lose weight if he were to live past forty five. I was in shock. Were these two quarrelling friends or enemies? I really couldn't tell. They left just minutes after they had arrived, leaving the three of us in a stunned silence, almost as though a mini tornado had swirled through the bar leaving a path of destruction. I honestly wondered if my new work colleagues, who I now knew were called Vijaya and Sujith would make it home alive.

"Well, I guess we've seen it all now. The *vagina* monologues," said Malcolm, and the three of us exploded again with the splendidly unstoppable laughter that one craves for at every good social occasion. Most of this laughter was pure shock from Daniel and I at what Malcolm, who was my new boss, had said. From now on, 'Vijaya' would be known as 'Vagina', and although at the time I thought it extremely unfortunate and cruel, I would very soon learn that it was the very least that this spelk of a man deserved.

Chapter 6 – not even a multipack of socks

Friday, 14th October 2016
Kandy, Sri Lanka

By the half term holidays, we had already visited Negombo, climbed Sigiriya rock, and visited Trincomalee in the North East of the island. The beauty was that almost every day, we were learning something totally new in an environment that was, just a couple of months earlier, completely unknown to us. Back in December 2014 we had been to Thailand for two weeks, and although we had indeed enjoyed it, there didn't seem to be quite as many differences that were as overwhelming as here.

One of first things that we had learned was not to be shocked when seeing drivers taking a swig from an alcohol branded glass bottle. When I walked into the staffroom on the morning of my first day at school, I was surprised to see that bottles of whisky, wine, vodka and gin littered the teacher's desks – in a country where drinking alcohol is quite frowned upon, particularly for women. I honestly thought there had been a wild office party, and was secretly disappointed when a colleague explained that everyone uses nice glass bottles to drink filtered or boiled water from as they don't trust the quality of plastic bottles.

An element of body language that we were quick to learn was the head wobble. What on earth does it mean?

When I asked, no-one was really able to tell me. The gentle wobble from side to side can mean yes, ok, maybe, or go on then. I must admit that I have now adopted this from time to time, purely to witness the priceless reaction of shop assistants whenever I come back to England. Another hilarious incident where body language highlighted the cultural differences between Sri Lanka and the UK was when I witnessed a small dunch close to my school. Two rather dilapidated vehicles had collided, and as a result the road was blocked in both directions. Furious beeping ensued, and my driver Gavesh had taken the initiative to resolve this problem. I felt obliged to assist him. As Gavesh extended him arm, flapping his hand up and down, I took this as the gesture for 'go away' or 'shoo!' "Gavesh, what are you doing? They need to start coming this way, they can't go anywhere else!" I cried. To my bewilderment, the traffic meandered towards Gavesh as though the magnetics had changed from repel to attract. After experiencing the results of this hand gesture a few more times, I learned that when a British person indicates to someone to leave something, or to go away, they may in fact be telling a Sri Lankan person to come right over.

As with schools and many other institutions, post offices in Sri Lanka are from a different era. For one, they still use metal weights which I found wonderful – in the UK one has to pay for a ticket to the Beamish Victorian

Village Museum to witness something like that! When posting letters and postcards to my loved ones, I was very surprised when I was stopped frantically by the postal worker when I licked the stamps, ready to stick them onto the letters bound for home.

"No licking stamps Madam!" she blurted out.

"But why?" I asked. She thrust a jar of glue and a brush at me, and motioned for me to paint the back of the stamp and stick it onto the postcard. Although the post offices are very different, the red post boxes are interestingly very similar to those in the UK, many still complete with colonial era branding.

Certainly one of the less quaint things about Sri Lanka has to be the abundance of powdered milk. This abomination of the dairy industry is served along with tea and coffee daily in the staffroom, complete with clumps of the powdery delight hovering hazardously in your morning tea or coffee. Fresh and good milk is available but a lot more expensive, and therefore less people tend to buy it. On the subject of dairy, there is also 'Astra butter', which I call '*Disastra* butter.' Again, because it is the cheapest option, many bakers use it in their cakes and pastries, which render them virtually inedible. Luckily, the Sri Lankan 'Highland' brand produces good fresh milk and butter, and is readily available in supermarkets.

Previously, I had complained tirelessly about the automated self-service machines in UK supermarkets. I also do not miss the security guards and their ninja-like obsession with fining anybody for parking in the parent and toddler bay just to use the ATM for two seconds. However once I experienced supermarkets in Sri Lanka, oh how I wished with my heart's desire to hear the words 'unexpected item in the bagging area' again! What a joyous moment it would be! The main supermarkets in Sri Lanka are Keells, Arpico, and Food city, which is affectionately known by my close friends as 'Food shitty'. I disagree with this slightly that it should in fact be called 'Food fishy', as every miniscule aisle reeks putridly of rotting fish, which is left out on the counter from the delivery in the morning for however many hours or even days until it is sold. The sales assistants are very friendly, and even friendlier if I ever buy a bottle of wine, when they are convinced I am having a party and hint at an invitation.

Before moving to Sri Lanka, I read that to drive here, it is imperative that you have the following three things: A good horn, good brakes, and good luck. There has never been a truer saying. Buses hurtle towards you at breakneck speed, often in the middle of the road as they overtake, regardless of how minimal the space between the oncoming vehicles might be. This was calmly explained to me as 'the middle lane.' Tuk tuks pull out directly in front of you with no warning at all, and I have to hand it to Sri Lankan drivers that their reaction times are exemplary. Perhaps their safety is truly insured after all from the dangling limes and chillies which hang from the bumper of many vehicles, which many believe will protect you on your journey.

One reason that I have chosen to stay in Sri Lanka for so long is the bus music. Speakers line the baggage racks, and the front of the bus is often adorned with eccentric flashing lights, a Buddha statue, Hindu Gods and incense sticks. They also often have beautiful flowers smartly draped across the front, bizarrely accompanied sometimes by teddy bears. The music itself is like nothing you've ever heard before; a wild 'rackety tackety' beat which persists triumphantly for as long as the bus driver requires, which can be four hours, or six, depending on the journey.

Monkeys are not cute. I was warned, but I foolishly refused to listen, and so I paid the price. They steal anything they can, including your washing, and proceed to throw it all over the neighbouring rooves. I also found that giving a pet animal a human name is seen as very rude in Sri Lanka (though it may be acceptable if referring to the name of a politician, who are utterly despised by every Sri Lankan person I have met to date).

Although I found the fact that Sri Lankan people will simply end a call as soon as they have obtained whatever information they require quite bizarre at first, I now really like the simplicity of hanging up the phone as soon as the conversation has ended. No more taking another five minutes to say goodbye and painfully extending a conversation which has already finished. A typical example would be: "where are you? There? Ok, coming." *Beep.*

Some cannot move away from the reliance on toilet roll, however the bidet shower, or more affectionately known as 'the bum squirter' by my friends and I is more environmentally friendly and in this heat, outright refreshing. I was told by some that the previous director of the British Institute in Sri Lanka loved the bum squirter so much, he took one with him back to the UK!

The most useful thing I had learned by this point, and maybe ever, was the phrase *'polimak tienneva!'* (There is a queue!) Pushing in front in a queue in a train station or in a shop is seen as a completely normal thing in Sri Lanka (and Asia in general I believe) which can be very hard work!

One of the strangest things to get used to, but by far one of the best things in the world, is having curry for breakfast. In all honesty, I don't think I will ever be able to eat another breakfast again without craving for the array of brightly coloured and delicious curries. Breakfast usually comes in the form of a bowl of *parippu* or *dhal* (lentil) curry, a bowl of fish or chicken curry, accompanied by *pol rotti* (thick round discs made with grated coconut and flour), as well as string hoppers, which are similar to noodles made with rice flour. There is also *kiribath* which is rice cooked in coconut milk and served in squares. The essential dish to go alongside every element of a Sri Lankan breakfast is the *sambol*. Sambol is a mouth-watering blend of scraped coconut, chilli, onion, and lime juice, and there are endless varieties. It sounds very basic, but it really is one thing I can no longer live without.

I had shared some of these stories when we met some of the British Institute teachers in Kandy and a group of retired Brits who were well known as 'the colonial wankers.' They had rubbed Daniel and me up the wrong way from the start at a house party organised by one of the British Institute teachers. One tall and rather angular looking lady had asked,
"How can you possibly be from the north, and hope to teach? I do pray you're not teaching English!" She had sank into her chair, smirking, surrounded by guffaws of triumphant and malicious laughter. They were not my kind of people at all, and had no desire to befriend any more 'expats'. I really hated using the word 'expat'. Why is it that when people from different countries come to Europe they are referred to as immigrants, yet when people from Europe relocate elsewhere, we are known as 'expats'?

And so, I began to learn some of the local language, which I felt was essential if I were ever to be able to integrate properly and make a friend circle which was more diverse.

My Sinhala teacher was the sister of the school receptionist, who had kindly agreed to spend one afternoon with Daniel and I a week so that we could hopefully at least learn some of the basics. She was a kind and meek woman who reminded me a lot of Professor Trelawney, the Divination teacher from Harry Potter, blinking behind huge glasses which magnified her eyes. She had the complete innocence of a gentle and frail old lady, and I admired how serene and calm she always was. Her name was Bujumbura. She had lived a fascinating life as a journalist and was very well travelled; and I was enthralled at the stories she had told of her experiences in so many different countries, from touring the saunas in Denmark to meeting Colonel Gadhafi in Libya! Although our allocated time for a class was just one hour, we would usually spend about triple that chatting away about the world and politics. I could see that after such a brilliant life she was now quite sad and lonely; a fate which happens to a lot of older and wiser people. My heart still sinks when I think about all those elderly people who are still so full of life with so many stories to tell, but there is no-one to hear them.

Unfortunately Daniel thought otherwise. He became increasingly frustrated and irate when I progressed much faster than him, and soon Bujumbura began to ignore him completely during the lessons, and we couldn't figure out what the reason for this was. We spent many an evening speculating and whittled our ideas down to two different theories. The first was that perhaps she was uneasy around men, which would be a valid explanation as she lived with her three other unmarried sisters. This was extremely rare, especially in

Sri Lanka, where if you were still unmarried after the age of 35 you were 'on the shelf.' The second theory was that she didn't wish to slow the lesson down and hoped that Daniel would catch up at home. This was also a possibility, and by the first half term break I had already witnessed that the attitude towards teaching in Sri Lanka was generally very similar to how it would have been in the UK in the 1950's: a heavy reliance on textbooks and copying and completing tasks in silence.

Bujumbura was a classic example of this, reeling off words as if in a university lecture, most of which we would probably never use (for example, elephant tusk). Nevertheless I noted down everything she said in a small white exercise book, grateful for the fact that her English was good enough to explain the meanings of the words, and she was one of the very few who were able to help us. I would practise with any Tuk Tuk driver or shopkeeper who would listen, and after six weeks I was able to at least give directions, ask for fruit and vegetables, and use numbers in Sinhala. Daniel had given up completely by this point, unable to retain any vocabulary at all, blaming Bujumbura's stand-offish attitude to him. He had now begun to refer to her quite viciously, and would ask: "You going to Bujumba-bitches house tonight?" I didn't say anything, as I couldn't be bothered for the confrontation, but I was starting to get really sick of Daniel's negative attitude.

I had settled well into my new teaching life at Thambili international school. We taught four languages; French,

German, Sinhala and Tamil, the latter two being the official languages of Sri Lanka as well as English. Sinhala was a beautiful script, and I often likened it to 'boobs and bums'. Tamil was more angular, like knees and elbows. Instead of the crippling 27 lessons a week I had endured previously, I now had just 18 lessons per week. The biggest class contained just 20 students, as opposed to the 36 unruly monsters I had had to contend with previously back in the UK. I now had so much more time to make sure that each lesson was excellent instead of the manic dashing around that I had enacted before, often resulting in lessons of haphazard quality. The atmosphere in the staffroom was calm, laissez-faire, and instead of having to stay at school until well after dark the majority of the teaching staff here were able to leave at 2pm.

Of course the facilities in the school, or the lack of them, had taken a lot of time to get used to. Instead of teaching using smart boards and power points, I had had to adjust to just a whiteboard and a pack of pens, and to classrooms which were completely void of any kind of technological or pedagogical resource.

The classrooms were dark and acoustically challenging, with cement floors and stiff metal chairs and desks; a world away from what I had been used to in the schools that I had taught at in the UK. I vividly remembered the expensive carpets, every classroom equipped with a computer with all of the state of the art software, a trolley of iPads, and an interactive smart board.

However, the results at Thambili International School were remarkably better than the absolute shambles I had battled my way through previously. Despite the catalogue quality facilities, the average GCSE results at Panaculty Academy had been meagre at best, with just 37% of the students managing to achieve a grade between A* and C in Maths. The English results had fared slightly better with 39% of students achieving between A* and C, which was a rather remarkable feat considering the rock bottom literacy level of the vast majority.

It was now clear to me that the answer to education was not to throw money at things, but to give teachers more freedom and time to plan their lessons as they knew best. I could now finally put the wonderful and engaging strategies that I had learned in my teacher training year to use, instead of having all of the passion and excitement stamped out of me by people who were completely monolingual and had never learned a single word of a foreign language in their lives. It was like watching a library being burnt down by people who couldn't read.

For a brief moment, I remembered my old Head of department, Louise Haughty. When I had begun my post at Panaculty Academy I had excitedly shown her some of my resources which had worked extremely well during my year as a trainee. Unlike the exceptionally open minded and enthusiastic mentor I had been gifted with during my teacher training placement school, Louise preferred to disregard any input I made completely.

"Speaking activities? Are you mad? This lot can't even articulate themselves properly in English. Plus Ofsted won't care about that. They want to see the progress in their books. Get them writing, every lesson. Without fail!"

"But that's so boring! However will we encourage them if we don't get them speaking and seeing what they can do once they try?"

Louise inhaled sharply and glared at me from behind her gold rimmed spectacles, clearly furious at having her authority questioned.

"This is our school. Our policies are not the same as where you came from. If you don't want to abide by them, then I suggest you go elsewhere. Ofsted is what is important for now, so focus on that. Honestly, the teachers that universities are producing nowadays are much less resilient. There's going to be a crisis soon, and it will be the experienced staff like me who will have to clear up the mess!"
She shook her head and returned to her marking, indicating that the conversation was over. She took a sip of her tea and I was disappointed that she didn't choke on it. Vile, vile woman. The pure hatred I had for her burned. I wanted to tell her that the younger

teachers at least knew how to use a computer, but I wisely decided against it. Almost as if she was asking for a fight, Louise spoke again.

"I completely agree with the approach of this school. If management use the 'beat with a stick' approach, then teachers don't get lazy. Especially the young ones who don't know the meaning of hard work."

I felt a plume of bile rise in my throat as I remembered that vulgar and inflated woman (inflated as in both ego and waistline). That day I had retaliated with, "well, it's like hoying cement on a new plant that is trying to grow. Doesn't really work does it?" Louise had shaken her head, and waddled away towards the den of senior management, probably to obsess over Ofsted, data, and targets.

I had bonded with my Year 7 and 8 students very quickly at Thambili International. They still had the innocence of childhood (which I find is disappearing earlier and earlier in the UK), yet they had a wicked sense of humour and were great fun to teach. I smiled to myself briefly as I remembered the lesson introducing the German alphabet with Year 7 a few weeks ago, and the students had been having particular difficulty pronouncing the letter 'ö.'

"Imagine you've just stood in something really, really smelly. Like... uuuughhhhh!"

"Ughhhhhhh!" the year 7s had chorused enthusiastically, before breaking into fits of laughter.

"Ich habe eine...Schildkröööte!" They echoed in unison.

(I have a tortoise).

The students and my new colleagues had responded very positively to my ideas for promoting spontaneous speaking in the classroom, and my new head of department, Malcolm, had even asked that I share my ideas with the other language teachers. I had enthusiastically reeled off all of the techniques that I had trialled and found successful during my year as a trainee teacher, and had then been instructed to lock them away and never to use them ever again by the evil of Panaculty Academy.

I began to feel particularly strongly about prioritising speaking strategies over grammar and writing in languages when I went to France after completing my A levels. I was barely even conversational in French at this point, and did not feel adequately prepared to begin a degree in the subject without doing something drastic to address my inability to speak well. I worked as an 'Au Pair' for three months, living with a French family who either could not speak a word of English, or simply didn't want to. At the beginning it was extremely tough, but after three months of total immersion I returned to England with a level of French which was astronomically higher than what I had achieved from going through the motions of the school system. The obsession with grammatical accuracy is what is destroying the confidence of any potential linguists before they've even begun.

I remember even in one of my first lessons of French as a Year 7 student, which was: 'Qu'est-ce qu'il y a dans ma trousse?' (What is there in my pencil case?) The teacher cared more about whether we got the masculine or feminine article (the 'le' or the 'la') correct than whether we had pronounced the words properly. This is where the negative cycle begins, and why so many young people are unmotivated to learn languages. When we learn our maternal language as a baby, first we listen, then we speak, then we read, and then we write. The grammar actually comes last. Yet for some reason, in schools we are trying to do it the whole other way round. Grammar first, writing, reading, listening, and then speaking comes last, despite being the most necessary skill for communication. The other issue of course is the very platonic and topics which are totally unrelated to real life scenarios, such as 'what is there in my pencil case?' During all my travels and experiences, I don't think I have ever needed to actually apply this knowledge in a conversation.

At Thambili International School, I had the freedom to teach languages in whichever shape or form my heart desired. Such freedom could also have its negative side however, for I was timetabled to teach A level German, which I was not really comfortable with as I was only really qualified to teach up to GCSE level at a push. In the end I succumbed and knew it would be better just to get on with it, but ask for support wherever it was needed. With my A level students I devised a great activity called 'diamond 9', designed to get them speaking. I gave each student 9 pieces of paper each with a statement written in German. The students had to arrange the statements into a diamond shape according to their beliefs, for instance the statements that referred the most closely to their personal opinion would go at the top, and those which did not at reflect their opinion would be placed at the bottom. At A level the syllabus becomes much more 'adult', in the way that the students must be able to speak about issues which are controversial for some such as right wing extremism, gay marriage, abortion, alcohol and drug use. Although students at Thambili International were generally very enthusiastic and getting the younger ones to speak was never really difficult, many came from very conservative backgrounds and it took a long time to coax the older students into feeling comfortable enough to discuss such issues at A level. The main problem was that they just didn't know what to say, which is understandable if they come from a strictly conservative or religious household where discussing something such as cloning is totally prohibited. These statements gave them ideas which they could then use and expand on.

During a Year 9 German lesson at my new school, we were practising asking "who do you get along with...?"

in German. Each student was given a grid entitled, 'find someone who…' and in each square there was a different question, for instance: 'Who gets along with their mother?' or 'who doesn't get along with their cat?' The students had to ask everyone in the class these questions and complete the grid with the name of any student whose answer related to each question. Within minutes, the atmosphere in the classroom lit up brightly, buzzing with enthusiastic echoes of „Kommst du gut mit Madu?" "Kommst du gut mit deiner Mutter?"

However when I stopped the students and explained to them that they were in fact saying: "Do you come good with Madu? Do you come good with your mother?" raucous laughter exploded, with many students burying their faces in their hands.

"You see how silly it sounds? Be careful! Don't forget the *aus* at the end, as it changes the meaning of the entire sentence from 'do you come good with…?' to 'do you get along with…?' „Ich komme gut mit meiner Mutter aus!"

Needless to say, I never heard the students make that mistake ever again!

I had been told never to use dice at Panaculty Academy, as Louise had stipulated that by using them you were asking for behaviour problems. Although it was true that they could well cause a dice war zone, I always felt that if I had been better supported with the behaviour issues I would have been able to teach much more fulfilling lessons. We were always told to adapt our teaching to plan for the behaviour of the students, but I'm sorry. Call me old fashioned, but no teacher should have to do that. We have to do enough as it is. The students are there to learn, and if they don't cooperate that should be their responsibility. We are raising a generation of young people who cannot cope if they are held accountable for their mistakes and they are very happily playing the blame game, because the system is allowing them to do so.

I began to use dice again at Thambili International, and they work like a dream helping students to remember new vocabulary. When I was discussing the weather with my Year 7 French class I drew a simple grid on the board, numbered 1 to 6. Next to each number was a small drawing of a different type of weather. In pairs the students would roll the dice and whichever number it landed on would dictate the type of weather that they would have to say. The quickest student of the pair would get the point. The classroom was quickly filled with cries of "Il pleut! Il fait beau! Il y a du vent! Il fait froid! Il fait chaud! Il y a des nuages!" *(It's raining! It's nice! It's windy! It's cold! It's hot! It's cloudy!)*

Prior to releasing the dice I had really enjoyed practising the pronunciation with them. It is no secret that French pronunciation can be extremely difficult. The two simple tricks are to praise the students for their successes, however small; and the second is to make them laugh. If you try to recall your clearest memories, they are usually of times when you were laughing. "Imagine the clouds are being sick, and the vomit is the rain! Il plurghhhhh!" I almost had tears in my ears from laughter as the students happily mimicked being sick, whilst perfectly pronouncing something they did not know ten minutes before in French. I was really beginning to fall back in love with teaching again.

Prior to leaving for Sri Lanka my mum had warned me that by teaching in a private international school I wouldn't actually be helping anyone, as the students at Thambili International would be from rich and privileged families who could afford the best private tutors. They would likely follow in the footsteps of their parents and go on to study in the US, UK, or Australia to become doctors, lawyers, pilots, or engineers. One of our new Sri Lankan friends Subashi had told us that many parents felt that any career outside of these fields would result in being 'a disgrace to the family.'

However it hadn't taken me long to work out that despite having everything they could possibly want at home; a state of the art television, a brand new Mercedez-Benz, and an in house cook and maid, quite a few of these children were very unhappy and for them, school was the highlight of their often lonely and boring lives. For some it was the only place where they could interact with other children. My thoughts turned to Dilshan Mawilmada, who was in my Year 9 German class. Although he was much more of a sportsman than an academic, his smile never faltered in lessons, and he enjoyed being in the class, enthusiastically joining in every activity as best as he could. His homework was not at all of a good standard, and once I had probed Mr Ranawana for details of his home life, I understood that it was because he had nobody to help him.

His mother worked abroad in the UK and his father in Saudi Arabia; and so on paper Dilshan lived with his 19 year old sister. However she was almost never at home as she was in Colombo studying at University, and so Dilshan spent his weekdays alone, with a maid to cook and clean for him. He lived in a beautiful, four bedroom house, complete with elegant balconies and ensuite bathrooms. Yet all this meant nothing when the beds were not slept in, and the grand dinner table was only ever set for one. Dilshan's situation was not unique. It was with great sadness that I also discovered Janaka who was one of my Year 10 students, living alone in a fancy apartment close to my house, with only a maid for accompaniment. I had always thought that being from a low income background was the most significant contributor towards poor behaviour and attainment back in England. However my opinion had altered within the space of eight weeks here as I realised that if children are denied the time, attention, and love that they so desperately need, money is in fact futile.

What was brilliant about having fewer lessons on my timetable was that I had time. Time to chase students for missed work and for interventions, time to really get to know them and their abilities as well as I could. Time to plan much better quality lessons, and time to brush up on my subject knowledge.

Sunday, 16th October 2016
Polgahawela, Sri Lanka

So now here we were, on the other side of the world at a quiet station in Polgahawela, about to catch the night train to Jaffna, the most northern city in Sri Lanka. It had been off limits for visitors for many years due to the war, and had recently opened up again within the past few years. The train was due to arrive and we waited patiently on the edge of the platform.

At 10.30pm the train pulled in, rudely disrupting the pleasant silence that had calmly enveloped the station just moments earlier, dramatically honking and belching smoke as though it was angry at having been stopped. Oh the effort! We boarded the train to be greeted by friendly, albeit many very drunk men who were smoking and clutching bottles of *arrack*. "You have to get off and go along to the first class carriage," said one of the men. "This is third class. People like you can't be in here." "Can't we get through this way?" I asked. The man shook his head and motioned for them to do as he had said. As Daniel and I walked along the edge of the platform, we began to worry that we couldn't find our carriage. The worry turned to sheer panic when we heard the blast of the horn from the train once more, and the wheels began to turn! Daniel managed to jump onto the moving train, yet it was picking up speed and I couldn't jump.

"I'll break my neck!" I wailed. As the train began to get faster and faster, the rhythmic clangs of the wheels against the track matched with my repeated whispers of "shittedy shit...shittedy shit!"

What happened next was unthinkable, and would never, ever, *ever* have happened in Britain, or anywhere in Europe for that matter. The train screeched to a halt and the guard, dressed in an immaculate white suit complete with epaulettes, grabbed me by the arm, and hauled me aboard. He was so smartly dressed he made the captain of the Titanic look like a mere vagrant. Angered by the situation, surely at the stupid tourist who had now made his train late, he barked at us, his harsh voice accompanying the stern expression on his face. "Where are your tickets?"

Once I showed them to him, he sighed heavily. "You're on the wrong carriage."

"I know that!" I protested. "If the station had clear signs where to wait for each carriage along the platform, this wouldn't have happened!"

"You people are bloody useless. You can't manage anything without a sign telling you where to stand, what to do, what not to do. How do you even drink water, without a sign telling you how to bloody do it?"

I would normally have argued back, but he had stopped the entire train for us and so reserved the right to be grumpy. As we settled into our seats for the long overnight journey up to Jaffna, Daniel whispered, "I don't think they would have stopped the train for a Sri Lankan would they?" As disgusting and unfair as it was, I knew deep down that he was right.

Friday, 2nd January 2017
Heathrow Airport, UK

Not even five months after we had left for Sri Lanka we found ourselves back in the very same corner of Heathrow Airport again, more than eager to return to our new tropical island home.

It had been a real pain in the backside having to fly into Heathrow. After that excruciatingly long journey all we had wanted to do was get straight to bed, though an eight hour bus journey up to Newcastle had lain ahead of us. Perhaps the horrendous journey had been the first sign that we shouldn't have come back. We really hadn't wanted to, though both my mum and Daniel's family had put so much pressure on us to return, and neither of us could be bothered for the persistent guilt trips that would inevitably come should we had refused to oblige.

It had been a horrible Christmas, the complete opposite to what both of our families had endlessly promised. Daniel's family had completely ignored me, despite it being our first Christmas as a married couple. They hadn't even made much of an effort with Daniel. It was perplexing how they had made such a song and dance about us coming back, and now it was almost like they wanted to punish us both for having moved away.

Soon, vicious arguments began to erupt between Daniel and me. I couldn't understand why his mother and sisters continuously treated me like a smear of dog excrement in the corner of the room that should be avoided at all costs, and were unpleasantly rude. Even my poor mum had come over to pick me up in the car and when we had invited her in for a cup of tea, she had of course smiled politely and asked how the Christmas shopping was going. Instead of responding warmly like any normal human being would, Daniel's mum chose to ignore my mum, instead sitting coldly in the chair opposite and fumbling with some of the grandchildren's toys. She clearly disliked my mum even more, possibly for the fact that she had produced me. Once we had got out of that stifling atmosphere, I had exploded at Daniel for not challenging her behaviour and allowing her to be so rude not just to me, but to my mum as well. Was she going to be like this for all of our lives!?

Daniel continued to make excuses for his mother and sisters, often saying that they were maybe 'stressed with work' or 'stressed with having all of the children now it was the Christmas holidays'. I would argue back saying that this was absolutely no excuse for their rudeness.

Daniel would then retaliate with the fact that he was getting drama from them about spending too much time with other friends and my family, and that I should understand he was caught in the middle. In a desperate attempt to try and resolve this recurring situation I decided to make a special effort for them, remembering my grandma's wise advice: "give people food, and they will like you." I carefully handmade each member of the family a card, including all of the grandchildren, and baked homemade cookies, which I placed in 25 pretty purple muslin bags, one for each member of the immediate family. Once they were all ready, I secretly blessed them with love and hopes of reconciliation.

On Christmas day however, my hopes were squashed completely. The children took one glance at the cards to see if there was money inside, and then with clear disappointment threw the cards in the bin. They found it more beneficial to stamp and smudge the cookies into the carpet rather than eat them. Not one person said thank you, but rather complained that they had wanted iPads. All of the other wives and girlfriends were gifted lovely spa and make-up box sets complete with a twenty pound gift voucher for the Eldon square shopping centre in Newcastle.

When I opened my present from his whole family to find a pair of pound land socks, this time Daniel was defenceless. A single pair of socks and not even a multipack can you believe?
There really were no more excuses he could possibly make for them. We didn't speak much in the couple of days before we returned to Sri Lanka where I would

begin the second academic term. There was nothing for him to say.

Chapter 7 – Ravindu, the sun and the moon

Monday, 9th January 2017
Kadugannawa, Sri Lanka

Ravindu rubbed his eyes ferociously as he continued to stare at the computer screen, wondering what else was possibly going to go wrong for him. After everything that had already happened, now the computer decided it's going to give in to the blue screen of death?

He had brought the wretched thing back from Australia just a few months ago, and it was pretty much brand new. Yet now, it seemed like it was yet another thing that he was about to lose.

At least he still had the house. It was a peaceful place, spacious and tucked away in the jungle, surrounded by coconut palm and mahogany trees which were so tall and strong they provided plenty of shade to keep the area beneath them relatively cool, even in the tropics. Monkeys roamed freely amongst the trees, picking fruit as they wished – though this was part of a regular pillaging that Ravindu intended to prohibit, as their numbers were growing rapidly, and they were becoming a real menace. They had already destroyed his water well by throwing in as much dirt and rubble as they could possibly find, as well as all of the discarded fruit which they would often so considerately take just

145

one bite from before they threw it to the ground. The amount of fruit that was available for him to sell decreased as fast as the monkey population increased, and it certainly was something to be addressed in the near future.

Yet now there was this computer to think about. He would have to try and find somebody to come and have a look at it in the morning. Though he wanted to fix it now, as he couldn't sleep. He couldn't remember the last time he had slept, or even ate a proper meal. And he was so tired of being lonely. It was his birthday tomorrow, and it would likely be little different from any other day. He had invited a few of his friends over, and asked if they wanted to share a bottle of *arrack,* but they were all busy with their families.

He paced up and down, trying to think of something else to do. His house was desperately bare, apart from a worn and torn (though still comfortable) red cloth sofa, a wardrobe, a yoga mat, a bed and the now broken computer. Ravindu had become accustomed to sleeping on the yoga mat however; as he had fallen into the pattern of watching a film or two before he could drift off to sleep. It was the only way he could numb his mind. The only item present in the house that bore any relevance to his life was a framed photo of his father when he was younger.

It pained Ravindu to admit that he was now totally lost. All of the effort he had made to get to Australia, and now he had returned back to his homeland it seemed as though it had all been for nothing. He had followed the path of so many other Sri Lankans; used up almost all of his father's savings and taken loans to make the journey to Australia to study for an IT degree, he had begun to earn a good salary and sent it back to his family, and had managed to uphold the reputation and glory of his family name for a couple of years. Yet now here he was: parent-less, wife-less, penniless and hopeless. A wrecked ship in a motionless sea, with no idea of which one of the prevailing winds would take him in their direction.

Although Ravindu had been born into a good family, from Kandyan 'high society', he had never accepted the class system and his position within it. His name meant 'the sun and the moon' in Sanskrit, which quite accurately represented his character. He was the sun in the way that he loved his life and showed great happiness for the simple things within it, and the moon in the way that he had a sad past, and at times felt very alone in a blackened sky. He was a source of light which people would gravitate towards and in other ways a total rebel. He recalled one instance from when he was younger, perhaps 11 or 12, when his household had been the only one in the area with the luxury of having a television set with a Nintendo games console. In his youthful innocence, he had warmly invited the other children from the village to come and play with him. They had excitedly agreed, pedalling their bicycles as fast as their little feet would permit to finally experience this magical box which offered games that were not cricket. Only as soon as they got comfortable on the sofa in Ravindu's living room, ready to start their gaming fiesta, his grandmother swept in, clad in a white sari ready to go and conduct her daily worship at the local village temple, furiously shooing them off the sofa like vermin.

"How dare you bring these low lives into our house? They are not of our status. Who knows what trouble they will bring? And they cannot sit on this sofa. I don't want to have to wash it again after having such low class sitting on it. Either they sit on the floor or they go outside."

It had greatly saddened Ravindu to see his good friends with whom he laughed with so often reduced to sitting on the hard concrete floor, just because they were not from a wealthy family.

"Sit on the sofa – don't listen to her. You are my guests and friends!" Ravindu's grandmother opened her mouth in protest, but was met with the sternest of glares from her defiant grandson. Unbeknown to him this was one of the many incidents which led him to become the man he was today.

Another time had been when he was slightly older during the school holidays. Ravindu had performed exceptionally well in his exams; and had been awarded a scholarship to a very reputable school in Colombo, and so he spent the majority of his teenage years in the school hostel unless it was the holidays, when he was allowed to return home. As a vast expanse of land surrounded the house which Ravindu's father had built, such essentials for Sri Lankan cooking such as jackfruit, coconut, durian fruit, guava, and mango were plentiful. This attracted many from the village, who earned very little and had large families to feed. On sighting anyone walking in his jungle, Ravindu would wave, smiling and gesturing towards whichever tree the villager was approaching, assuring them that everything on his land was to be shared. That was until his grandmother caught him, and scolded him harshly.

"Those are our trees, and our fruits! They'll come and take them all!"

Although Ravindu had been subjected to this behaviour and classist way of thinking from a young age, he always refused to accept such heartlessness.

"You call yourself a Buddhist? You go to the temple and listen to the monks who teach us Buddha's words of how important it is to give, but then you don't want to give in reality?"

He may have lost the respect of his family for his insolence, but this had never bothered Ravindu. He was his own person, who followed Buddhism in the way he felt was right.

Ravindu did not regret his sudden decision to return from Australia, although it was difficult for him to accept that so much had gone wrong in just two years.

He had been so eager to follow many others like him out of Sri Lanka, to experience the free western culture and to finally be able to earn a good salary and the respect that would come with it. He had begun his degree at the Queensland University of Technology; studying what many other Asians were famed and headhunted for: Information Technology. Although he had made a promising start and was scoring well on his assignments, he was working a total of three jobs in order to pay his way through university and send money home to his father in Sri Lanka. As a result he wasn't able to eat or sleep properly, let alone have any time to make friends or socialise, and he was running on about four hours of sleep a night. The time difference also meant that he was unable to keep in touch with anyone in Sri Lanka, which included his friends and his wife, whom he had married the day before he left for Australia at the request of her parents.

He had heard so many good things about Australia; the towering skyscrapers, the immaculately clean streets, the brand new cars and the highways, the high salaries, and he had expected to have all of this and be happy. He had not anticipated that in fact the opposite would happen, and that he would in fact end up so lonely, cold, and depressed. He hadn't realised he was in such a bad way until his university lecturer had noticed his persistent absenteeism and had taken him to one side and asked if he was alright. When she discovered that he was not alright, he was referred to the campus counsellor. The sudden death of his father had been the last straw for Ravindu, and he decided to give up the chance of obtaining permanent residence in Australia like the hundreds of thousands of Sri Lankans before him, and return back to his homeland. The 'western dream' had not materialised for Ravindu, for it was not material things that would make him happy, but the love of others.

He now found himself worse off financially than ever before, selling coconuts from his land and teaching English and music for the poor children from the village in order to survive. He refused to work for anyone else again. In Australia the money had been good of course, so the enslavement of working long hours for a faceless organisation was bearable. In Sri Lanka however, the minimum wage was so diabolical that he could not understand how anyone could sell themselves for so little. It was like corporate prostitution. For instance, a typical office job requiring someone to work 40 hours per week would pay around 25,000 rupees (approximately 125 pounds) per month. Ravindu liked maths, and it only took him a few seconds to calculate that the minimum hourly wage was around 150 rupees (80 pence). Perhaps it was some of Ravindu's 'proud high Kandyan' upbringing that was finally beginning to make an appearance, or maybe he was more wary, having done the whole chasing after money thing in Australia already and having suffered from it. For now, he was content to live the simple life in pursuit only of things that he had a passion for, such as music, which was a life that few understood.

Chapter 8 - Slightly Chilled

Friday, 17th March 2017
Kandy, Sri Lanka

After the first time that I saw him from afar I knew that I would always remember him, down to the finest detail. He stood at such ease in front of the punters in Slightly Chilled, one of the only establishments in Kandy where one could enjoy a beer in a place with some atmosphere. Many were in high spirits, possibly because they were enjoying St Patrick's Day in the heart of a tropical paradise rather than on a rainy Dublin street. The first ten weeks of term had passed so fast, and the Easter holidays were just around the corner. Our friends Sally and Manuel were coming to visit us and would be arriving in a couple of weeks.

I chanced another sneaky side glance at him again. Though not the tallest man I had ever met, he certainly was dark and handsome. His curly tousled hair was thick and black, and gleamed with almost a hint of blue in the light. His skin glowed with the health of a tropical diet and plenty of Vitamin D from the ever present sun, a sultry burnt cinnamon bronze. His nose was broad and his lips thick and full, but what I really couldn't take my eyes off was his smile, which could easily be the envy of any Hollywood actor or actress. People paid thousands of dollars for veneers in the hope of obtaining perfectly straight, bright teeth, and I knew of so many young girls who were almost bankrupting themselves for lip fillers. This guy had it all naturally.

However I couldn't describe this guy as 'Hollywood.' Hollywood is usually better known for its fakes, its plastic surgery trials and successes, and mishaps of course. Nothing about his smile was fake at all; the way it spread all the way across his jaw to highlight the gentle warmth of his melted chocolate eyes. He also sported a designer beard which I had observed was a typical trend in the south Asian region, and it neatly framed his face with razor sharp precision.

I chanced a look at him again, and this time he caught my eye. More than that, he looked straight back at me, and smiled that oh so pleasing, 'I want you right now' sexy smile. Or was he just being friendly?

After all as a musician, it was clearly in his interest for people to like him. I was sure that he had plenty of groupies anyway. As he spoke softly into the microphone, I did not hear his words, for I was too overcome by his voice. As the band broke out into 'Paradise' by Coldplay, the echo of his voice soothed me like the feeling of a warm relaxing bath. The very sight and sound of him had brought me such comfort and pleasure, though I didn't even know the guy. I was happy with just looking at him. For all I knew, he probably knew how good looking he was and was an egotistical maniac.

As the melody of the acoustic guitar continued to be well received by many in the bar, I was perhaps too visibly moved by the seriousness and passion in his face as he played. It was so different to the cheeky boyish grin that I had just witnessed moments earlier, yet his serious stance was equally as pleasing. I had attracted the attention of my friend, Subashi, who I noticed all of a sudden was looking disapprovingly at me.

"They're great, aren't they?" I grinned, in an attempt to cover my tracks by selecting the word 'they' instead of 'him'. Subashi shifted her thick purple rimmed spectacles and cleared her throat.
"They're ok, I suppose. Average. Though Colombo bands are much better. There's no place for musicians here in Kandy. And they'll earn nothing, I bet you."

Subashi worked as an English teacher at the British Institute in Kandy and, as she often pointed out, it was like being colonised all over again. They had even made her work on the 4th February, which was the Sri Lankan Independence Day, when everyone else in the country had the day off!

Jokes aside, she earned an enviable salary with numerous training opportunities – she seemed to be doing a different qualification almost every month. She frequently described herself as a coconut whenever we encountered somebody new.

"I'm brown on the outside, and white on the inside." She would boast proudly. She had unicorn coloured curly hair, of which I was immensely jealous, and a vast array of tattoos. She spoke with an accent so articulate even the Queen of England herself would be queuing up for elocution lessons.

Our other friend Alina was seated next to Subashi. Like me, she was from Europe, but from Slovenia. During the past few months, I felt as though I had learned almost as much about Slovenia as I had about Sri Lanka. Being from a nation of only around two million people, it seemed that Slovenians were very proud of where they came from. Not unlike the Geordies in the North east, who are both well-known and feared for their fierce regional pride. Alina spoke with an American accent with a strong Slavic tone, and was certainly never shy to let someone know if they had displeased her. She had straight red hair and was married to a Sri Lankan. Malcolm and Daniel were also present as well as Alex, who taught at the Alliance Française in Kandy. Although he was French, he had lived in Dublin for many years earlier and spoke with a strong Irish accent. I could have listened to him for days on end.

Although we could all wind each other up at times, the three of us girls were firm friends. We were so engrossed in our conversation about when we were going to have our next cooking club and which country we would choose as our theme this time that we didn't realise that the music had stopped. The two band members, who had been strumming along and singing heartily just moments ago, were making their way towards the table where us three girls were sitting. Some of the local boys eyed their rival predators with jealousy as they stalked their prey. As the majority of Sri Lankan women anywhere outside of the capital Colombo didn't go out, let alone drink, Kandy's few drinking establishments could sometimes be more like a scene from one of David Attenborough's documentaries when birds are desperately trying to find a mate for the season, proudly puffing out their chests and doing crazy dances.

"Good evening. I hope you have been enjoying the music," said the musician at whom I had stared for half of the evening. As we stood to greet them he moved forward to kiss each of us on the cheeks. 'Oooh, very sophisticated,' I thought. I guessed that he had perhaps spent a lot of time in Colombo, which was now very westernised. The other guitarist said nothing, preferring to caress his mobile phone almost as affectionately as he had his guitar.

"I'm Ravindu, and this is Ruwan. But just call me Ravi. And you all are?"
As we chatted, I discovered that he had indeed grown up in Colombo, in a hostel. His English was good, with just a smattering of mistakes. His voice was smooth and thick like chicken liver pâté, and I was about to suggest that he should record mantras, for people to meditate

to if the whole band thing didn't work out, when I had an idea.

"Can you play any Sinhala songs?" I blurted out.
"Of course!" laughed Ravi. "Which one do you want to hear?"

"Not hear. I want to sing!" I flushed, emboldened by the few Lion beers I had already consumed. I had learned a Sinhala song at school in preparation for the carol service back in December where the teacher's choir had sung one song in English, and one in Sinhala, dressed elegantly in saris. As a practising Catholic, Malcolm had done a reading during the service, and when the lines 'and God came on all of them' were read aloud, Daniel and Alina, who had come along to watch, burst into fits of laughter which had echoed all around the church, causing parents and Mr Ranawana to turn around and glare in disgruntled rage, and for me to cringe in my church pew, mortified.

Needless to say, like me, Daniel and Alina were not at all religious. For the majority of Sri Lankan people, the idea of not having a religion was incomprehensible. Gavesh had once told me that having no religion was like having no identity card or morals. I often humoured the open mouthed reaction of shock horror whenever I was asked: "Which religion are you? Christian?" and I would respond honestly with "I'm atheist".

The way people reacted if ever I told them that my parents didn't get married until I was four years old was even more hilarious. I remembered how last month, I asked Gavesh to give a lift to one of the very traditional sari wearing teachers from our junior school to the main road. Her name was Indrani. The driver, Gavesh was having a chat with her about how white people often lived together before they married.

"And sometimes, they even have children without even being married! The crying shame!" Indrani shook her head in disapproval. I couldn't believe it. Like Mr and Mrs Nugawela, this woman was a teacher in an international school! How could she be so narrow minded? I wanted to see how she would react to me.

"Well, I was 4 when my parents got married. I've managed to turn out alright enough!" Indrani had gazed at me in absolute shock, her mouth hanging open in horror. When I had continued, "does that make me a bad person?" her mouth remained wide open.

This was a similar reaction, particularly from the local Sri Lankan crowd, when I sang in Sinhala a few moments later. Once I finished the popular song 'mal madahasa peedana' the audience, who had sat in stunned silence during the song, stood cheering! I had never experienced a reaction like that before. People asked for me to sing again. They took photos and videos on their mobile phones. They asked me to pose for selfies with them. It was overwhelming, and I realised there and then that maybe I could revive my love of music that I had forgotten and pushed aside so many years ago. It was such an electric and addictive atmosphere that night, which surged through my veins like a current even when Daniel and I arrived home later that night. I was absolutely buzzing with energy. I wasn't at all prepared for what came next.

"You're an attention seeking little slapper, you know that? All those guys drooling over you. And you posed for photos with them and led them on. You loved it! And you just ignored me. How do you think that made me feel? I feel like a mug!"

I hadn't expected this, and I didn't want to hear it. Daniel had always been so calm and easy going, and had never once tried to control me or dictate to me how I ought to behave. I would never have allowed that and he knew it. I felt so irritated that he had now ruined what had been such an unforgettable night. He knew how much misery I had been through, and how unhappy I had been. Surely any normal husband would have been happy for me?

I quickly glanced at my phone. It was a Facebook request and message from Ravindu. *'You were amazing tonight. You reminded me of Adele! There's no expiry date for you if you want to join with us again. Cheers.'* I shut off the screen quickly before Daniel could see.

"I'm sorry you felt like that. Why did you wait until now to say anything? You've never gone on like this before!"

"I absolutely hate it here Lilee. I'm bored out of my mind."

"People have tried to help you to find work. You always turn everything down!"

"Because the salary is rubbish! It's a joke. This country is a joke. I've come here with you this year. I choose where we go next year. Hand your notice in."

"I'm not leaving! I'm happy here! What, you want me to go back to the misery we came to get away from? No way."

Similar conversations and disputes continued and steadily increased in frequency over the next few weeks, and as the weeks turned into months, Daniel's mood became gloomier and gloomier. I began to dread coming home from yet another great day at school and walking into the living room, to find Daniel sitting shrouded in darkness, with the curtains still shut at 2 in the afternoon and surrounded by several empty beer cans. The room stank of stale beer and smoke. He had made no effort to learn the language, or embrace the country in any way at all; preferring to wallow in self-pity and anger that he had come to the other side of the world only to end up defeated and jobless.

I did feel bad for him, but the continuous cycle of negativity and pushing anyone who tried to help him away was becoming too much to bear. As he swore and snapped and whinged about the meals that I had often spent hours cooking even though I was the one who had been at work, I wondered if I loved him anymore. Or if I ever actually had. Had he just been a close friend and a drinking partner all this time?

Saturday, 22nd June 2017
Kandy, Sri Lanka

Following my debut as a Sinhalese singer in Slightly Chilled back in March, I had clung on to Friday nights as the anchor to pull me through the working week and my rapidly disintegrating marriage, though I was in between trying to pretend it wasn't happening, and putting it down to just being a rough patch that all marriages go through. Nevertheless, I really looked forward to every Friday night singing with Ravi and Ruwan. We soon began to attract a lot of attention, and it wasn't long until total strangers began to recognise me in town not as the international school teacher, but the Friday night lounge singer.

Today was 'la fête de la musique' which was a small scale music festival organised by Alex at the Alliance Française de Kandy and I had been asked to recruit Ravi and Ruwan to play the opening set. Finding enough acts who did not suffer from stage fright was a challenge, as well as the fact that many students had been forbidden to come to the festival by their parents, for the sole reason that it happened to take place in a bar. We had practised a couple of days prior at our house, making sure that we had a good variety of songs in Sinhala,

English and French to fill our thirty minute set. Daniel had sat moodily in the corner glued to his laptop, preferring not to support us or encourage us in any way. I had been shocked when Ruwan had pointed out that he had seen a girl with ginger hair the previous Friday night in Slightly Chilled, and proceeded to ask me nervously:
"can boys have red hair too?"
"of course! Prince Harry, Diana's son and the Queen's grandson, has red hair."

Although there were a couple of students I recognised from school in the crowd, I hid behind the bar so that I could sneakily down a Lion beer before our performance. It went really well, and Ravi had recorded the entire set and had planned to edit it and publish it on YouTube in order to gain more publicity for the band. I was gutted that Ravi and Ruwan had to leave straight after the festival however, as they had another gig to play that night. After they had gone, Alex, Daniel, the French teachers and I partied way into the night, until one of the drunken local guys got a bit too carried away with Charuka, one of the female teachers, who understandably got quite upset and batted him away, when he retaliated quite nastily.
"He said I'm not Sri Lankan and I'm behaving like a whore, drinking and dancing and all that."
Daniel had approached the drunken idiot and demanded that he should apologise, however the

scrawny scumbag had other ideas, and swung a punch instead. Big mistake.

Daniel retaliated with maximum force, and was met with a counter attack from scrawny and all of his friends. Alex and the male French teachers joined Daniel's side at once, and soon what had started out as a tame music festival became a full scale brawl. Interestingly, the sleepiest and quietest towns can have the most intense dramas.
"New York may be the city that never sleeps, but Kandy is the city that never wakes!" Ravi had said once.

Once we got home, huffing and puffing about the night's events, I checked my phone to see a couple of messages from Ravindu.
"You bring so much energy to the place when you are there. You light the whole place up."

Chapter 9 – Camp in a castle

Saturday, 19th August 2017
Niederalfingen, Germany

I had found employment for both Daniel and I over the summer holidays on a summer camp in south western Germany, which had proven to be hard work, yet rewarding. As well as wanting to keep my German up to speed, I had researched far and wide to find and secure this job for us both, in an attempt to lighten Daniel's spirits, and also provide him with some work experience and a chance to earn money, which would hopefully bring him some self-satisfaction that he had not had for almost a year.

The camp itself was run by a couple who had been together for about 6 years and were about to get married in the September. Their names were Carrie and Tim. They ran language camps regularly in Scotland and also in Germany and were very successful. Carrie was a qualified languages teacher from Scotland, whilst Tim was German. Carrie always wore long denim dresses and wore barely any makeup, and I thought she was naturally very beautiful. Tim was very German looking, with a very pointed chin and steely eyes. We had flown into Stuttgart airport and taken the train to the small town of Aalen as instructed, only to arrive at the station and find that the payphone was broken, and neither of our Sri Lankan phones were working, even though they had done in the UK at Christmas.

"Now what are we going to do? Yet another place you've brought me that is a total nightmare!" Daniel began to kick off and I couldn't be bothered for another one of his meltdowns. I ignored him, leaving him to light up a cigarette, which he puffed on angrily. A couple of young teenagers were standing not far from the phone box. Surely they wouldn't mind phoning a German number?

As soon as I asked, I realised that I had forgotten how we in Europe are now raised with this terrible fear of talking to strangers, particularly if they are asking for something. 'Never talk to strangers' we are firmly instructed by our parents from a young age. As I began to explain the situation to the two teenagers in German, and asked if I could make a quick call on their phone so that we could be picked up by someone from the camp, they shook their heads and avoided any eye contact before walking away. I decided to try the café opposite the train station. Again, I was cut off by a 'nein danke!' *(no thank you!)* before I even had a chance to say anything. Feeling increasingly desperate, I looked to the left to see a small restaurant, the panelling adorned with Turkish script. There was nothing or no one else around; it was my only chance. As I entered, a short Turkish looking man appeared at the counter.

"Ich liebe türkisches Essen," I babbled. "Ich komme nicht aus Aalen und mein Handy funktioniert nicht – können Sie mir helfen? Ich muss meinen Freund anrufen, weil ich total verloren bin!" *(I love turkish food, I'm not from Aalen and my phone is not working – can you help me? I have to call my friend because I am totally lost!)*

I blabbered fast, hoping that he would hear the pleading tone in my voice and listen. Smiling, he handed me his phone, indicating which button to press to make the call. How kind! Why had it been so simple for this man to help me, yet for the other people I had asked, it was an impossible task?

After a half an hour wait, we were finally met by two men in their late twenties or early thirties, who introduced themselves as Tim and Lucas, who was another worker at the summer camp. We bundled into their car, the exhaustion from the journey hitting us, and were chatting for a few minutes before we pulled up in a large underground car park.

"I thought the camp was in a castle?" I inquired nervously. This looked a bit dodgy.

Tim laughed loudly and smiled widely.

"You didn't think we were going to let you both start without an initiation, did you? We are in Germany. Let's drink some beer!"

We walked down the pretty cobbled streets of Aalen to see a group of people of a similar age to us sitting outside with some very tall glasses; the pints of beer that you don't get anywhere else except for Germany. I looked around and took in the delightful surroundings; crowds of young and middle aged people sitting outside, chatting excitedly and laughing together under broad parasols emblazoned with different brands of German beer.

I felt almost as though I had 'reverse culture shock' as I noticed all of the women and men enjoying themselves, drinking and laughing together. The street was immaculate, the buildings were topped with quaint and dainty rooves, and the hanging baskets laden with brightly coloured flowers complimented the array of chalkboards on which offers of food and drink were written. With a slight pang in my chest I realised just how much I had missed the freedom of Europe, the vibrant social life and the wonderful variety of food and drink. Although I adored my job and my students in Sri Lanka, as well as my new circle of friends and the dependable warmth of strangers, towards the end of our first year there it had become increasingly irritating to be stared at as though we were aliens, and thought of as 'bad' if I was seen drinking a beer, or god forbid, had a cigarette. I settled with ease in my chair as we were asked to join the group, feeling that this was going to be a very well-deserved working holiday that we would both enjoy.

Three of the other camp mentors, or *Betreuer*, were German: Tim, Fabi, and Pia, then there was Carrie, Tim's fiancée, who was Scottish, and two were American; one of whom was Lucas who had come to pick us up from the station with Tim. The other was his soon to be wife, Kelli. She was also a non-native teacher of German in the US. Everyone seemed very friendly, and were all returning for the summer having already worked on the camp for the past couple of years. We were the only newbies. As Kelli began to reel off everything that we would have to do in the morning before the children arrived, I began to feel overwhelmed. It must have shown on my face, as she grinned in that typical American way, and said:
"It's going to be just fine. Just join in with some games of *Völkerball* and it'll be totally sweet!" Despite trying to

be encouraging, she still hadn't managed to shift the look of confusion on my face.

"Völkerball? Never heard of it!"

I would soon learn that it was a cousin of the game 'dodge ball', played on a basketball court where there were two teams, and each team had 'kings' who had to stand outside the perimeter of the court. The other players on the inside of the court had to pass the ball to their 'king', who would pelt the ball at players of the opposite team in order to get them out.

Four weeks passed in the blink of an eye, and both Daniel and I had really enjoyed living in the small, yet magnificent castle which had been our home for that month. It had been wonderful waking up to the homely smell of freshly baked German bread and Pretzel every morning, and having delicious meals cooked for us all three times a day. The kitchen ladies were lovely, even the one nicknamed 'the dragon' by the other mentors, who told us how she had terrorised the staff and children with her ferocious temper last year. I had found her very nice indeed.

Both Daniel and I had settled quickly into the routine of the day: to conduct a ten minute fitness warm up session for the children after breakfast, teach an English lesson from 9 in the morning until midday, and then help lead the afternoon activities after lunch. After dinner, there were also a variety of evening activities. It was extremely tiring and after just a week, I felt totally burnt out, trying to catch a twenty minute power nap wherever possible. Although we were both enjoying the new experience, and learning new activities that we could both use with students in the future, I came to realise that I was not really enjoying the teaching part in the morning. Many of the children were unmotivated, and would have much preferred to be outside in the beautiful summer weather playing Völkerball than being stuck inside learning English. I sensed that many of the parents had sent them here to occupy part of their long summer holidays and also so that they could have a break. The lessons themselves were very engaging and well planned; every day would be themed on a different topic.

On Mondays, the topic was fashion, and so I would introduce clothing vocabulary and the students had to create their own outfits using the dressing up box which was kept in the castle, before choosing a model to parade down the corridor and the other students would narrate their display in English.

On Tuesdays, the lesson was themed on sport and fitness, and so was usually more popular with the sportier members of the group. I would introduce and practise sport and fitness vocabulary with the children, and then prepare a script for a fitness video, which we would then film outside in the castle grounds. The students breathlessly explained the different activities in English as they ran on the spot, did squats, push ups, skipping, or stretches.

Wednesdays were the best, where we did film making. It would take the whole morning lesson for the students to prepare their scripts, what each person would wear, where they would film their different scenes, and what props they would need. The afternoon was spent filming, and we watched the films once Carrie and Tim had uploaded them all on the Saturday, which was the last day. We used iMovie on the iPads to film, complete with an array of funny sound effects. Some of the ideas were absolutely hilarious, starting with a version of Harry Potter where Voldemort was Voldeclingy, and was madly in love with Harry and wouldn't leave him alone (instead of trying to kill him persistently like in the real films). There was also 'Burned,' instead of 'Frozen', a version of Star Wars where Darth Vader was a harmless geek instead of an evil death lord, and a version of Cinderella where she didn't lose her shoe at the ball, but her mobile phone, and the prince searched for the girl whose thumbprint would unlock the phone instead of the original 'whoever the shoe fits' story.

On Thursdays, we would learn about food, and create disgusting recipes and design the menu for a restaurant that surely would not gain even one star on Trip advisor. Each week brought different creations; from watermelon omelette to onion chocolate cake, ketchup ice cream and slug salad garnished with nail clippings.

On Fridays, the last full day of the camp before the children would return home after lunch on Saturday, we would learn vocabulary about houses, and then students would get to work designing an ideal house in space, ready for when, if ever, Richard Branson does manage to launch his space travel company. There were some great ideas, from installing a button which would change the entire colour of the house, to strawberry ice cream flavoured walls, to beds made of jelly and a floor which could turn to lava and incinerate any trespassers.

On Saturday morning, the campers would pack and check out of their rooms after breakfast, and fill out their final entries of their camp diaries, which they would have 15 minutes to complete every morning before we began our English lessons. Some children would complete these meticulously, writing an animated account of their day, including plenty of adjectives and presenting their diary entry very well. They would also add beautiful drawings to illustrate the exciting day that they had had previously. Others would roughly scribble a barely legible sentence, and knowing that parents would undoubtedly want to read these in order to evaluate how well their child had progressed in English, I would insist that we would not continue the lesson until they had completed their diary entry properly. This led to a spat with a student named Hermann Schwarzkopf - a name so German I had only ever expected to come across it in a German textbook. He crumpled the diary and threw it on the floor, folding his arms.

"This isn't what I came to this summer camp for. I want to play table tennis."

Having experienced nothing but the grace and enthusiasm of Sri Lankan students for a year, I was no longer prepared to deal with bad behaviour. I honestly hadn't had one incidence of bad behaviour the entire time I had spent so far at Thambili international school. I could just teach as creatively and passionately as I wanted, without having to worry about discipline. The parents did all the discipline for you and the job was infinitely easier. I had come to realise just how unnecessary behaviour management was, and that we as teachers should not be frightened to stand our ground in the fear of angry defensive parents or management with no spine.

"Tough. And if you show such disrespect again, you can sit in your room all afternoon." Hermann fell quiet, frowning, and I noticed a few students with their mouths hanging open and nudging each other. I hoped that I wouldn't be in trouble for this, as I knew it was a summer camp, not a school environment.

Unfortunately, my instincts were right. Later that day, Carrie took me to one side before we were due to have dinner.
"Lilee, can I have a word?"
I knew already that it would be about this morning's incident where I had threatened Hermann with solitary confinement.
"You can't speak to the children like that. They pay a lot of money to come here, and we rely on their parents to send them here year after year, and spread the word so

that we end up with more campers. If word gets out that the children feel like they're being bullied by the staff, we're finished."

I could see Carrie's point of view, but I stood my ground.
"So we just tolerate insolent behaviour then? If the others don't see action being taken, they will all follow and do the same!"
"Maybe Hermann felt...a little bored?" said Carrie tentatively.

'Oh no no no,' I thought. 'Not this all over again'.
"I followed the instructions that I was given, that they start each lesson by reflecting on their previous day and completing their camp diaries. Isn't it strange how he was the only child who had a problem with that, and all the others were perfectly happy to take a pride in their work? If we send him home with no diary, or a diary that you can't even read, surely his parents are more likely to complain about that?" I reasoned. Carrie pondered for a moment, before waving her hand to show that the conversation was over, as she wasn't getting anywhere.
"Let's just agree to disagree then. It's not worth a conflict. Just be careful not to speak too harshly to the children."
I opened my mouth, ready to protest at how ridiculous this was, yet she was already walking away.

I felt angry that I was from a continent where I felt I no longer belonged. I could not, and would not, accept this 'blame culture', where nothing is ever the child's fault, even if they behave appallingly. How on earth are such children going to deal with real life, when they will just simply lose their job? No employer would ever put up with this. But yet again, as it had been in the UK, it seemed very much that the problem was me. I shook off my thoughts quite quickly, as I had plenty of more pressing issues on my mind.

I couldn't help but worry as I reflected on my feelings. I had completely fallen out of love with Daniel and I knew it. The whole time that we had been in Germany, I hadn't stopped thinking about Ravi, feeling excited if I saw there was a message from him, and disheartened when there wasn't a message, or if he took a long time to reply. I knew that it was wrong, and that I had to stop it, but I couldn't. The fact that Ravi had gone a bit quiet on me over the last few weeks should have helped the situation, though it was making me want to hear from him even more. I had constantly told my friends to "stop being silly" when they fretted about someone they liked not messaging them back. Now I understood how they felt completely. I racked my brains, trying to recall a time when I must have felt such obsession about Daniel in the early days, I *must* have done - but my mind was blank.

I couldn't even remember the last time that we had had sex and I hadn't just lain there waiting for it to be over –

it had been months since we had even done anything. It was awful that I could not pinpoint the reason for this change, and it wasn't that Daniel wasn't attractive; he was tall, muscly and strong, and prided himself in the hours he clocked up at the gym in order to keep up his enviable physique. I just wasn't attracted *to him*. It was becoming clear that we had comforted each other and enjoyed each other's company, but I was fast learning that desire is not something that can just be switched on like a light bulb. I was now noticing only his imperfections, his tantrums, his irritability, his rudeness and his ignorance towards other people.

The camp itself was very well organised, and there was also the trip to the adventure park once a week, which was the highlight of the week at camp for most of the children. The downside was that, if you worked at the camp and were slightly afraid of heights, you had to accompany the children on the high rope courses. There were about seven different high rope courses, all varying in degree of difficulty – from red (easy) to black (very challenging). I had profusely stipulated that I would be able to manage the red, orange, yellow, blue, and green courses, but not the purple or black ones. However, after much egging on by the children, I regrettably ended up on the black high rope course.

"Shiii-tzu!!" I screeched, trying my hardest not to swear as my feet slipped from the speedily swinging plant pots and I fell, suspended by my harness, bouncing uncontrollably up and down. This particular part of the

175

course was very high up, and although I was protected by the harness and carabiner clips, I felt extremely unsafe and exposed.

"Heeeeeeelppppp! Hilfe!" I could see the campers on the safe platform ahead, doubled over with laughter. Miriam, one of the girls, managed to ask if I was ok. "Neeeeeein! Hilfe!!" I shrieked in despair. Not only was I terrified that the harness could tear or break at any second, but I was now also absolutely mortified, and my face was bright red with a second layer of embarrassment over the primary layer of sunburn. As one of the adventure park workers came to my aid, I descended, my head in my hands, discarding this day as one that I would much rather forget.

Other excursions on the camp included a trip to the local *Freibad,* or outdoor swimming pool, and a 'bad taste party', where there was a prize awarded for the worst dressed camper. With so many activities, the four weeks on camp passed in a blur. Just one thing remained sharply wedged in my mind, something that could not be blurred out at all.

Daniel and I had bickered continuously from starting the day at breakfast, right up until we had gone to bed almost every night after a few beers with the rest of the staff. I hated the way he had begun to speak to me, about me, and about Sri Lanka and its people, in the unpleasant mumbling drone of his voice. One morning at breakfast, he mumbled "pass me the juice." I couldn't quite hear him and had asked him to repeat, which he did, snarling through gritted teeth. "Pass me the juice, you stupid-"It was then that I decided that I had had enough, whether it was in front of the others or not, and snapped.

"Don't speak to me like that!"
The others exchanged awkward glances, but continued eating before changing the subject. I couldn't speak to anyone about how I felt, not even my closest friends. I knew that it would all be talk of "it's a rough patch" or "my mum and dad went through this" etc. The fact that we were married made it all a huge mess. It wasn't as simple as just ending the relationship normally as you would if you were girlfriend and boyfriend. No-one was ever going to advise me with what I wanted to hear.

After weeks of hard work and keeping up pretences with Daniel, the last of the children were safely returned to their refreshed-looking parents. Along with the other mentors, we were now free. Now that we had the entire castle to ourselves, were getting ready to party to let off some steam and say good bye to each other properly.

Music blasted, drinks were plentiful, and spirits were high. It had been a fulfilling four weeks for sure, and I was very grateful for the experience and all that I had learned. But I could not relax, and my smiles weren't genuine. I poured myself a glass of wine and took myself out of the room, so that I could collect my thoughts for a moment. Although I felt panicky and unstable, I determined that whatever I felt towards Ravindu was a silly crush and it would blow over as long as I avoided him once we returned to Sri Lanka tomorrow. I had married Daniel, and up until they had moved away everything had been fine - in terms of their relationship at least. Telling myself that everything would be fine and that I was being daft, I joined the others upstairs just as the party was getting into full swing. I drank until I saw double and passed out in bed at around one in the morning.

When I woke up the next day, Daniel still wasn't there. At first I thought nothing of it, and that maybe he had ended up passing out somewhere random and we would all laugh about it later. I did think twice however, when I went down for breakfast and everyone was already sitting around the table with bread, ham and cheese, everyone that is, except for Daniel and Pia.

Chapter 10 – Plugs and Parades

Monday, 25th September 2017
Kandy, Sri Lanka

We returned to Sri Lanka at the end of August, and nothing much had changed. I had happily settled back into the routine at school, and Daniel had been offered a post teaching English at a school in Kurunegala, about a 40 minute commute from Kandy. Although I had thought that this would boost his spirits and improve his morale he constantly grumbled about the low salary, and sometimes stayed in bed in the morning, saying he couldn't be bothered with the bus journey and he wouldn't be going into school that day. What he said about the low salary was indeed true: he was only to be paid 1,500 rupees per day, which would work out at around 30,000 per month. (In pounds sterling, this would be roughly 7 pounds per day or 150 pounds per month). About ten per cent of this would be spent on his bus fare daily, and everything else would be his to keep. It had been a real struggle to encourage him to take the job. What he failed to understand despite being told repeatedly was that 30,000 rupees was the average salary of a Sri Lankan teacher in both government and international schools, and they usually all had a degree.

As I returned yet again from school to find Daniel slumped on the sofa in darkness, the floor littered with beer cans and cigarette ash, the curtains drawn despite the lovely sunshine outside, I could not hide the upset in my voice. I still had not confronted him with my suspicions about Pia in Germany. I had decided not to at the time, as I didn't want to burn any bridges with Tim and Carrie in case we miraculously patched things up and wanted to return to work on the summer camp again next year. Even though we were far away back in Sri Lanka now, Daniel's mood swings were so volatile I couldn't be bothered for any additional conflict, so I kept schtum.

"You didn't go to school, again!? And how much have you wasted on beer? It's a flipping Monday!"
Daniel exploded at me, his face blotchy with fury and contempt.

"That salary is a disgrace! I'm not working for that."
"Daniel, that is the average salary here! That's what teachers here earn, and they even have degrees! Many earn even less than that. You don't even have A levels. You can't expect to earn a high salary with no qualifications!" I ranted at him, waving my hands, exasperated.

"I'm a native speaker, which tops any qualification they have, especially from these Mickey Mouse universities here. They're totally crap, which is why so many go abroad. They should be much more grateful to have me. Like Malcolm said, they're monkeys. Fresh out of the jungle. They still don't know what civilisation is. We have to teach them, and they should be much more grateful."

I was ready to explode at this ugliness. I wanted to bash his stupid gammon head against the wall, and knock this ridiculous over inflated ego out of his body. How had I never noticed this horrible side of him before? Had it always been there, or had it just appeared recently? I wasn't sure. I couldn't believe that this who I had married, a gammon in hiding who believed he was superior because he was British and white.

Unfortunately so many of them didn't die out in the dark ages, and continue to haunt us all. It was with regret that I realised this was one of the attitudes I despised the most, and I could never love anyone who had it. For how long had Daniel had this attitude? How long had it lurked there like a festering disease? I wanted to argue, but I knew as long he was in this mind-set it was pointless. I decided to change the subject in the hope of brightening this rapidly souring atmosphere at least slightly. Though my efforts were to no avail.

"I tell you what. Why don't we invite Alina and Sanjit over for dinner tonight? It might do us some good to be around friends at the moment."
Daniel made a rude sound.
"And have Sanjit drink all our beer again? No way. Stop inviting people for dinner man. How many times do we get invited elsewhere? Way less than the amount of times you invite people here. And your friends are weird anyway."

I plodded into the kitchen, defeated. I was so sick of him pushing away those who had tried to help him, and throwing everything back in their faces. Nothing was ever good enough, and it seemed the thought of money was the only thing that would ever make him happy. Daniel's complaining continued for weeks. I said that maybe he should go back to the UK for a while, as he was a misery here. In all honesty, I wanted him to go and leave me in peace, and it had got to the point where I was much happier at work than at home. It felt like tooth decay; the erosion had previously lain unknown below the surface, eating away. Now it had reached the root, and the realisation was as painful as I anticipated toothache would be. As my mum and brother Bert were due to visit in the October break, I hoped that they would bring some distraction and normality. Distraction they brought, normality I'm not so sure.

Monday, 23rd October 2017
Kandy, Sri
Lanka

After my mum and brother's arrival, we had spent a couple of days around Kandy, and Daniel had been very good, taking them around as I was at work until the afternoon. Tonight we were at a housewarming party, which had been organised by Beverly or Bev for short, who was an English teacher at the American College. Once we had arrived, to my utmost dismay and secret happiness, I noticed that Ravindu had also been invited. He looked amazing, in a tight fitting purple-grey floral shirt, though he was definitely much skinnier than I had remembered before we had gone away to work in Germany for the summer.

Due to the heat, mum had barely eaten anything, but it hadn't stopped her consuming almost three bottles of wine. If we had all been at our apartment it would have been fine (or maybe not, due to our extremely nosy landlords) however we were a short journey from the house by road, and she was already swaying drunkenly to the music, yelling:

"get some bloody real music on, not this mainstream crap!"

My brother and I were mortified as usual when mum got drunk around people who didn't know us too well. So far, she had insulted the director of the British Institute in Kandy by calling him a wanker, purely for the reason at him having been living there for four years and having done nothing to resolve the street dog situation. It was heart-warming how passionate mum felt about the numerous dilapidated street dogs wandering the streets; often stick thin with protruding ribcages, and covered with mange and scabs. However, attacking the director of the British Institute whom Daniel had hoped would help him find a much better paid job was not the way to solve the issue. I have to admit that I had found it secretly hilarious as I'm sure everyone else did, when the director had backed away, his nostrils pinched, his face exuding the expression of absolute shock and horror.

"Golly – I dare say, I haven't been called a wanker for about thirty years, since I was at university!"
His words failed to stop mum. He had no idea how to deal with a drunken northern woman with a bee in her

bonnet.

"You're a wanker. WANKER! 4 years… and you do nothing… look at those poor animals! I hope you choke on your fancy buffet lunch while you're spending your massive salary on *yourself,* instead of being of any benefit to the world." Mum strutted away, before tripping over and crumpling in a heap on the floor and bursting into manic laughter. I saw that Ravindu was looking and buried my head in my hands. Even for western culture I knew that mum's behaviour was extreme, but I was pretty sure that Ravindu would probably never have seen a drunken woman at this level before. As everyone stared, Ravindu's grin didn't fade at all from his face, before he gently hoisted mum up by her arms and took her into the spare room to lie down. He stroked her hair and made sure she had water and was sleeping, before returning to the main gathering outside.

"I'm so sorry," I said before cringing, planting my head in my hands. "I don't think she ate anything all day. She can be a bit crazy, but her heart is in the right place. If you're a genuine Buddhist, you can't judge anyway! Though you're already drinking, and you've eaten meat, which you're also not supposed to do!" Ravindu laughed.

"Don't worry. Under all that craziness I saw a very sweet person." His voice was so soothing and calm, and washed over me like a warm monsoon rain. He looked right into my eyes for a moment, and neither of us said a thing, just held each other's gaze. He began to say something, and then said the three worst words that exist in any language: 'it doesn't matter.'

Everyone was in a real party mood, even though it was a Monday night and a fair few people had to work the next day. By two in the morning only Daniel, Ravindu, me and my brother were left. As I collapsed onto the spare bed which I was to share with Daniel, I clung onto Ravindu's words as they began to slip from my conscious memory. "I wanted to tell you something, but...it doesn't matter." Did he have any idea how annoying it was, to say something like that!?

I was awoken at six the following morning by someone tapping on the window. It took a couple of moments for me to get my bearings and remember where I was. It was Ravindu tapping on the window. He must have stayed on the sofa, I thought. Daniel was still fast asleep, and I didn't wake him, as I was going to work and he was to take my mum and brother up into the mountains today. I was doubtful that it would happen. I crept outside and chatted for a few minutes with Ravindu before insisting that I jump in the shower quickly before I went to work. Ravindu offered to drop me on his motorbike. As I clung onto him for dear life as he weaved in a suicidal manner through the sea of Tuk Tuks in the morning traffic, I was alarmed to feel his ribs prominently through his T-shirt. "You've lost loads of weight," I murmured. "Is that a good thing?" he replied, grinning boyishly as always.

I somehow got through the day at school, although the heat combined with dehydration convinced me that I was going to pass out during Year 9 German. I also nearly managed to electrocute myself when plugging in the CD player so that I could conduct the listening activity. In Sri Lanka, it is like a lottery when it comes to plug sockets. Some are the two pin European style, some are the three square pin British style, and some are a round three pin style, which is a different thing entirely and can be assumed as being the Sri Lankan style. Many of the classrooms at Thambili International are fitted with the round three pin sockets; however our department CD players have the European two pin plugs. In order to get around this obstacle, we were told simply to stick a pencil or pen in the top hole in the socket, and then slot the remaining two pins in, et voilà. As an unqualified electrician, I found this move both enthralling and terrifying. Sometimes plug sockets happen to be in really illogical places as well. I recall one instance when Daniel and I stayed in a hotel near the airport in Negombo, which was well equipped with a kettle, however the socket was halfway up the wall towards the ceiling, meaning that Daniel had to hold the kettle up in the palm of his hand as it boiled.

When I returned home, I returned to an empty apartment. It turned out that mum, my brother and Daniel had been successful in their mission for today. I checked her phone for the first time that day to find a barrage of messages, one of which was from Bev, which I thought was unusual as we were not particularly close.

"So stuff kind of happened between me and Ravindu last night. He's hot, huh? I figured you're quite good friends with him aren't you. Could you find out if he's interested? I'm going to go and watch him play his gig on Wednesday and see if he wants to start dating. I never saw this one coming, but hey I'm certainly not complaining!"

I wasn't sure why, and it was definitely far from reasonable, but I felt my insides churn up a cocktail of both fury and shame. I wasn't just angry, but livid at Ravindu for being a tease and leading me on, yet I felt ashamed at even having these feelings in the first place. I was married, and Daniel was currently tour-guiding for my family even though everyone was hung-over. I decided to make myself feel relieved that at least, now Ravindu was off the market, and the whole 'falling for him thing' had been totally stupid. Thank goodness.

"So you and Bev hey?" I sent a message to Ravindu with a winky emoticon. He replied within seconds, almost as if he had been waiting for my message. I opened the message to find the emoticon with the thin horizontal line, and then the blushing embarrassed emoticon. "Well you had Daniel."
What on earth did you expect?! I wanted to say. I had an inkling of what he meant but decided to ignore it completely.

"Do you like her or was it just a party thing?" I had to ask.

"A party thing..." he replied. "I never thought it would happen...I should text her shouldn't I?" I couldn't tell whether he was telling the truth or not.

"*What!?*" Mum had exclaimed when they all returned from their day out, and she had overheard me telling Daniel about Bev and Ravindu's passionate encounter. Daniel had been thrilled and shocked at the same time, exclaiming:

"but Ravi is *hot*. Bev is.....*not*. These Sri Lankan guys will just take anything they get, won't they? Just like the street dogs, they'll just take whatever they find. No standards! See, I'll only have the top fillet steak of the highest quality." He moved to put his arm around me, and I flinched. This nasty attitude again. I did not like it, and I no longer welcomed physical contact from him.
"A fillet steak? So I'm essentially a cow then, yeah?"

Mum was much less thrilled than Daniel.
"Do you know what, its people like her who give white women a bad name! That's why they all think we're easy, because of people like her throwing themselves at a bloke when they're too drunk to know what they're doing! And then they want respect? Pah!"
I was surprised at the intensity of mum's reaction, but secretly satisfied.

Friday, 27th October 2017
Kandy, Sri
Lanka

On the evening of Mum's birthday, we headed to Slightly Chilled where Ravi and Ruwan would be playing as they did every Friday night. Subashi and Alina came along too, and surprised mum with a bottle of red wine and a sari, which Alina wrapped around her. Compared to her previous performance at Bev's party, tonight she was calm and serene, and enjoyed a deep conversation with Joan and Alison, two of the new British Institute teachers who had just arrived in the past couple of weeks on a six month contract. They couldn't have been more different; despite being in her 40s, Alison was young at heart and also young in the face – she could have passed for a 20 year old! She was bubbly, animated, and full of life, keen to discover Sri Lanka and enjoy every opportunity. However Joan seemed to do nothing but complain, and compared the lower living standards in Sri Lanka to Dubai, where she had previously taught. I couldn't help but think that if she were not in her 50s, she and Daniel would have made a perfect couple with their incessant whinging.

Aside from Joan's complaints, everyone was in good spirits, and Michael, the owner of Slightly Chilled, signalled for Ravi and Ruwan to play 'Happy Birthday to you' as I had told him it was mum's birthday. Michael was tall and well built, and had a particular fondness of vests, which he wore almost every time we saw him. He was a very good DJ, and I always got excited when I saw him put on his glasses as I knew it was time for him to get the vinyl's out.

His gruff and outspoken character made him oddly likeable, and he was well known for retaliating viciously at anyone who gave him a negative trip advisor review. One particular example was when somebody had written a negative review which complained that the toilets smelled terribly, and Michael's response to this was: 'was that before or after you spent a penny?' There were no bouncers at Slightly Chilled, but Michael's two boxers, who could sniff out trouble when they were not sleeping. I recounted the time to the party at the table about when I had sang alongside Ravi and Ruwan once, and a very drunk local had decided that the music was just too sensual for him, and had begun to strip in the middle of the bar. The image of Michael grabbing the tiny frail drunken man by the collar, and the sound of Michael booming 'get aaaaaaaaat my pab!' resonated within me forever since. He was married to a very beautiful and quiet Chinese lady.

As mum downed her birthday shot which Michael had brought for her, the atmosphere in the bar was as electric as the guitars which were playing. I couldn't refrain from catching Ravindu's eye and when he grinned, it was as though somebody had implanted two magnets under my cheekbones, and I was smiling back. I caught myself finally, and prayed that no-one had noticed. When everyone left, Daniel announced that he was going for a drink with Alex.

"A bit of lad's time," he declared, smiling.

Mum, my brother and I headed back to our apartment, and cracked open the bottle of red wine which Subashi had brought for my mum. Once we had said 'cheers!' and took the first sip, mum caught me off guard.

"So are you going to tell me what's going on, between you and the band guy?"

Oh shit. *Busted.*

"What?! Nothing! Why would you even think that?"

"I think every single person in that bar would think that. The way you both look at each other...well there's definitely some pretty strong attraction."

"Ok, attraction, fine. That's all it is. Am I not allowed to appreciate the way people look?"

Mum cocked her eyebrow, leaned forward on her hands, and fixed me with an all-knowing stare.

"Just remember, I'm your mother. And I know you better than you think."

Friday 3rd November 2017
Knuckles mountain range, Sri Lanka

"Didn't you ride an elephant in the *Perahera* once? Sounds like you did it again the other night. We should call it the 'Perabevver' instead!" guffawed Angus.

The *Perahera* was a famous cultural event that took place in Kandy every year, complete with elephants adorned with jewels and beautifully embroidered material, parading alongside Kandyan dancers and drummers. The inclusion of elephants in the *Perahera* was becoming increasingly controversial; and very much like the arguments surrounding Spanish bull fighting or English fox hunting, many were of the opinion that having elephants in the parade was 'cultural' and therefore essential. However, I personally disliked the *Perahera* for two reasons; one being that I just found forcing elephants to march amongst hundreds, maybe thousands of people with fire, light, and chaos downright cruel, and the second reason being that they banned all alcohol and meat sales in Kandy for two whole weeks.

Of course, I understood that I had made the choice to live here in Sri Lanka – and therefore had to respect their customs and rules, but *two bloody weeks*, and in the middle of the school holidays, so I wasn't even at work! After being completely unaware of this and having experienced this first hand in 2016, from then on I had made it a point to make sure I was as far away from Kandy as possible when the *Perahera* was on. Kandyans from all walks of life would enthusiastically ask if I had seen the *Perahera*, their hearts clearly brimming with pride, and I would usually answer in a robotic fashion, 'yes, it's wonderful', rather than risk probable deportation if I were to tell them the truth about how I really felt about it.

I didn't expect Ravindu's 'Perabevver' encounter on Monday night had been quite as glamorous as his experience in the actual *Perahera* had been, although I didn't want to think about it any longer.

"Hey Angus, that's not nice." Ravindu replied in his smooth and sexy voice, but it had a tone of warning that Angus was going too far with these comments. Angus was a self-confessed posh boy, educated at an extremely expensive English private boarding school, and had no idea about reality and how not to insult people, especially the unfortunate – those unfortunate both financially and physically. He wasn't wrong in a way, Bev was enormous – they had invited her on this hike with them, but she had declined, probably preferring to sit at home gobbling her éclairs and wallowing in self-pity at having got it so wrong with Ravindu. She had gone alone to watch him play on the Wednesday night, and told him that she was on offer whenever he wanted. Ravindu had declined this lucrative offer. He had already seen all there was to her, and no air of mystery or lust remained.

Daniel had gone away for the weekend with Alex, who taught at the Alliance Française and was our friend. I had decided to join Ravindu and Angus, along with a group of others who worked with Angus at his school on a hike in the knuckles mountain range. We all laughed the entire way. After we had all set up camp for the night, we sat outside drinking the foulest, cheapest local gin (Ascot gin, which is certainly nowhere near as prestigious as the horse racing venue) and soda water (as Ravindu had picked up soda water instead of tonic) and played the guitar and sang songs. The moon shone, brighter than any streetlight, illuminating the top of the mountain so vividly that there was no need for a torch or mobile phone. By midnight Ravindu and I were alone.

Although I was still secretly livid with him for messing about with Beverly, the force of attraction between us was so strong it was like a live power line, suspended between two pylons. We chatted about this and that, enjoying each other's company yet skirting around what we both really wanted to talk about.

"I know this is wrong to say, as I don't want to disrespect the marriage. But I can't hide my feelings for you any longer," murmured Ravindu. My heart almost stopped.
"I feel the same… but nothing can happen. For now, I'm happy just to look at you," I whispered back, enjoying those moments while they lasted. I knew they couldn't happen again, although I was itching for them to.

Monday 6th November 2017

Kandy, Sri Lanka

Dread filled me as I waited in the living room for Daniel's return. Although part of me hoped that the fun weekend away with Alex had maybe cheered him up slightly, I knew that it would not be long before he inevitably reverted back to his irksome state of mind.

When he arrived back, he did indeed seem brighter and happier. As we sat out on the front porch that evening, sharing a cigarette, he spoke animatedly about his few days away. As he spoke, I realised that I could not stand his drawling, mumbling voice, and his boring conversation. The thought of lying next to him again that night repulsed me. I no longer wanted to share a house, let alone a bed with him. I wanted my own space.

Taking a deep breath, I pushed out the heavy words that would put in motion the next sequence of events. "It just feels like we're friends doesn't it? There's no love here anymore, is there?"
Daniel stopped in his tracks, and I felt the weight of guilt on my shoulders. He hadn't expected this at all, but a happy reconciliation after his absence.
"Well...yes, you're like me best mate. But it's always been like that. Maybe I should go and stay with Alex a few more days, so then you'll miss me." He laughed, his confidence returning quickly after the hit. Although I was happy that he had recovered quickly, I still did not think that this would resolve the problem. I felt racked with guilt and self-loathing for feeling this way; I knew it was wrong, yet I just did not enjoy his company any longer.

As Daniel left the next morning, I noticed that he hesitated as he ambled through the door. I knew that he was hoping that I would have changed my mind, and beg him not to go. I wished that I had changed my mind too, but I hadn't. After he left, I scrolled through old photographs of all our previous memories; nights out with friends, our holidays together, and our wedding photos. They were all evidence of amazing times which we had shared and enjoyed together once, and it was extremely sad to think that this journey may now end, and that there would be no more happy memories together. This chapter was finished, and the book was closed temporarily as I battled with my mind, unable to decide what to do next for the best.

I spent the next two days in the midst of this battle, and I decided to draw up a pros and cons list to help me predict what would come to pass should I have the guts to end the relationship with Daniel. If we had been only boyfriend and girlfriend, it would have been very simple – though marriage added a whole other dimension, and required a much greater level of consideration. In the end, I concluded that the main con was the worry of what other people would think. I was terrified to share how I felt with anyone, for the fear of judgement; though all this was such a mess, and so I had little choice. I arranged to meet Alina for lunch the following day.

We chose to meet at Cafe Banana Chill, which was owned by Viraj, a friend that we had made when we had attended a couple of Hip Hop dance classes in a desperate attempt to keep fit. Although it had been fun learning certain steps such as 'the cabbage patch' and the 'Steve Martin', my ability to coordinate my arms and feet at the same time had been totally abysmal, and the watchful eye of mobile phones were ever present, which would cheerily record my failings and upload them on social media. Viraj was a very talented dancer who had even featured in professional music videos, and it was clear that I would never be in the same class. Alina had excelled and picked up the choreography very quickly; though she had become too busy with her tourism company to continue participating in the weekly lessons.

"If I tell you something really bad, will you judge me?" I rested my head on my hand, feeling glum. Alina finished sipping her Mojito, which was very tasty, though it did in fact look more like a small garden than a drink.
"I'll tell you straight what I think. But it will stay between us of course."
I took a deep breath. I knew as soon as I told anyone how I felt, I was risking it being out in the open. I desperately hoped that the well-known saying 'if you tell your best friend, you tell the world' wasn't true.
"You know how you've been with Sanjit for like 9 years...in that time, did you like anyone else? Did the crush go away? How did you get over it?"
Alina smiled her all-knowing smile.
"Well, when I was away in the states, there was this

American guy. He was a musician, and I really liked him. We met a few times, but nothing happened. I knew that once I left, our paths wouldn't cross again. It's totally normal to be attracted to someone else. You can look, just not touch!"

"I know that's normal. But what if it's more than attraction? Like the thought of never seeing them again makes you actually feel pain inside, and every time you get a message from them, you stop everything you're doing to read it and reply, and when you see that they are 'typing...' and then they stop, it makes you want to smash something?"

Alina didn't stop smiling as I thought she would have done. What she said next stopped me dead in my tracks.
"It's Ravindu, isn't it? You've got it baaaaaaad."
Oh, bollocks.
"How did you know? I haven't said a thing to *anyone*."
"Are you mad Lilee? It's so obvious. The way you two look at each other...it would even turn a eunuch on."

"So what do I do? What can I do to make this go away? I've never felt anything like it, and it's scary!"

"Only you can make that decision, Lilee. No-one can do it for you. But I think you already know yourself. And maybe, you're actually in love for the first time in your life."

Friday 10th November 2017
Kandy, Sri Lanka

We had been back at school for the past three weeks, and the November exams were looming. At Thambili International, all students had to complete exams in November, and also in June. We also had to devise all exam material from scratch, and were not allowed to use material from past examination papers, in the very unlikely event that students would access them from the library, where both hard and soft copies were kept. Schools are very much like hospitals, in the way that each one has a very different way of doing things. In the same way that it's always good to get a second doctor's opinion, it's very likely a similar concept when it comes to teachers.

Two new teachers had joined Thambili International this term from London. Prior to Malcolm's impromptu departure in July, he had leant over his desk, and in hushed tones, informed me that they were married women.

"What a complete blunder by the management," he began to embark on yet another tirade, for which he was well known.

"The boss is in a right panic. What a total mess! These parents will be absolutely seething. I wouldn't be surprised if there's a mass exodus of students as they pull their kids out of the school. I mean what on earth were they thinking? Choosing to teach in a country where homosexuality is technically punishable by death, let alone being married!? Talk about not doing your homework!"

Unfortunately for Malcolm, it was times like these when his age really showed. He had been a great head of department, very welcoming, and at times very fun, but his archaic attitude towards the modern day world could be perplexing. I loaded my canons, ready to defend two people I didn't even know.

"It's an international school though. I think it's a good choice by the management. The majority of these children will go abroad for university, which means they will inevitably come across people from all walks of life. Surely as an international school, it's our job to prepare them for that? I'm pretty sure the students are much more aware about topics like same sex marriage than we realise anyway, with the internet at their fingertips. We discuss about same sex families in A level French and German anyway!"
Malcolm wasn't having any of it.

The thing was, that despite my chagrined defence of these two women I had yet to meet, on arrival they did not seem at all that keen to make new friendships here, preferring to head to Colombo every weekend to meet up with people there that they already knew from London. Although they of course had no idea of the discussions which had taken place prior to their arrival, I admit that I felt slightly let down by them. I had expected them to breathe a bit of fresh air into the place and be a bit more social, yet they had just buggered off every weekend. I suppose it was only then that I learnt one of life's many lessons: to respect the rule: 'each to their own.'

However, tonight was different. It was Audrey's birthday, and for the first time, they had invited us out in Kandy for a drink. Of course, they had chosen to meet at the most expensive location possible; at the same hotel where I had not so fond memories of tomato ketchup pasta with Mr and Mrs Nugawela after their laborious prize giving ceremony. After ordering a beer, I could then understand just why alcohol had seem so off limits the day of the prize giving ceremony – 1000 rupees (around 5 pounds) for a local beer! In a different situation, I would have commented that it was daylight robbery, but it was Audrey's birthday, and so diplomatically chose to remain silent, drink up, and enjoy.

Daniel and Alex were also present. It was now four days since Daniel had gone to stay with Alex, and I still didn't miss him, his alcoholism and his negativity at all. The subject of our separation was now hot gossip, and people eyed us awkwardly from each angle of the table. This became worse after he came to speak to me, and everyone instinctively leaned in the opposite direction, although it was painfully obvious that they were determined to crane in and listen. I wish they had.

"You know, I've done nothing but think these past few days. I haven't been able to eat or sleep." As Daniel began to speak, I felt awful at the stress that he was obviously under. He was wearing a plain white T shirt and jeans, and looked no different to when I had last seen him a few days earlier. Again, I began to feel repulsed at myself for feeling such a void towards him, when he hadn't behaved like terrible husbands do in most films, books, or TV dramas, and of course in real life. By that, I mean he hadn't to my knowledge murdered anyone, beaten me up or become domestically abusive. He hadn't been involved in a drugs heist, or robbed a bank or anything else unsavoury. He had been loyal and had risked his happiness and job to come to Sri Lanka with me, and I had friends repeatedly telling me how lucky I was; how they wished that they could find someone who would be prepared to travel with them. I looked at Daniel, desperately trying to feel the unmistakable gravitational pull that I had felt towards Ravindu. Nothing. He might as well have been a stranger. The sole consolation was that I had done nothing to denigrate his character.

"I realised that there's no explanation that there's someone else. So is there?"
Oh no. What on earth should I say? I couldn't lie, but I couldn't tell the truth either. But then what was the point of telling the truth if nothing had even happened anyway? Thankfully, Daniel spoke again before I could answer. I think my hesitation had spoken for me

anyway.

"The thing is, Sri Lankan women are just gorgeous aren't they? I mean you could never compete with them." He emitted a short blast of laughter. This was typical Daniel sarcastic humour. I let it wash over me, and rolled my eyes at his charm.

"I've actually been thinking that getting married was the wrong choice. We should enjoy being free like everyone else. I mean who else our age is married?"

I couldn't believe it. Was it possible that Daniel felt on the exact same wavelength as me?

"Yeah, I totally agree. Even the words *married, wife and husband* just sound god awful. I feel about 90 when you refer to me as your wife!" I laughed, easing up as this conversation seemed to be going much easier than I had predicted.

"Aye. And I've had so much interest you know. Girls throwing themselves at me. Pia from the summer camp. There's that English teacher from my school as well, Charanee. You know the one who made me that amazing birthday card in September?"

My mouth fell open in surprise. I hadn't even seen it. Yet now Daniel had mentioned it, it all made sense. The effort she had made for his birthday, Daniel's increased irritation and displeasure towards me, and the complete lack of any sort of romance or intimacy. He helped himself to some nuts which were in the centre of the table, and proceeded to talk with his mouth full.

"So basically, she's all over me. And asked me to come

over to her place soon. So maybe I will," he finished with his trademark jagged tooth grin. I glanced down the table. Everyone else was deep in conversation. I took a deep breath and began the last conversation we would have together as a married couple.

"Well, seeing as you've been honest, I might as well be. I think you should meet her, and see how it goes. I didn't want to be interested in anyone else, and I didn't think I ever would be, but life has its way of throwing things at you that you can't control." I noticed that Daniel was leaning forward in his seat, hanging on my every word.

"So who is it?" he asked. I teetered on the edge, still reluctant to say his name. I instinctively glanced behind me, in the direction of Slightly Chilled, where we all knew Ravindu would be playing tonight. Before I could say anything, I heard Daniel laughing as he stood up suddenly.

"I fucking knew it. Oh, you stupid, stupid bitch. You have jungle fever! I'm just going to pop to the loo. I'll be back in a bit."

Once Daniel had gone, Alex asked me how things were going. He listened with such intent that I'm sure he could have been a very successful marriage and relationship counsellor had he not taken up the post of director at the alliance française, and with his French-Irish accent people would surely remember him to recommend.

204

"So is everything ok now? All patched up?"

"Erm...not exactly." I mused. "Though I think we are actually on the same page. I don't think he thinks it was the best idea to get married either, and still wants to be free." I tried not to notice the confusion fleeting across Alex's face, but it was there.

"Well, that's not what he's said to me at all. He's been a real mess these past few days."

The sudden realisation of what was happening suddenly hit me like a sledgehammer.

"Shit, Alex – could you possibly check in the toilets and see if Daniel is there?" I pleaded. It was pointless; I knew already where he had gone. Alex looked at me, completely nonplussed. I tried to disguise the panic in my voice but it had already taken hold of my voice box. "I'm sure he'll be over in a minute. He's probably just taking his time."

I didn't hang about to convince Alex otherwise, but sprinted over to the men's toilets myself. I shouted Daniel's name, and was unsurprised when I heard no response. I turned to see that Alex had followed me, a bewildered expression on his face. Bewildered rapidly became discombobulated once Alex had searched the toilets and realised Daniel's sudden absence.

"Where do you think he's gone?" he quizzed. I let out a loud moan, knowing that in just minutes away, the cat was going to be out of the bag for all to see and judge. I sprinted over to the rooftop edge, sure to be well out of earshot, and called Ravindu. I had to warn him at least.

I was too late.

As I pulled my phone from my bag, I noticed a couple of missed calls and messages from Ravindu, reading:
'Why is Daniel all of a sudden here shouting, and saying all this crazy stuff?'
I felt absolutely mortified. Nothing had even happened between us! And now nothing ever would for sure. Maybe, I thought, I should just lead a celibate life after this, free from drama and complications. I pressed the call button, fearing the worst. I hoped that I was just overreacting; though I knew that Daniel was capable of serious harm, and Ravindu had little chance of defending himself, especially if he were caught off guard like this.

I remembered all too vividly one bitterly cold February night out in Newcastle with our friends, Sally and Rob. It was past one in the morning, or 'danger time' as Daniel used to say. "Nothing good ever happens after one o' clock in the morning." He certainly was not mistaken in this case. A man of rather formidable grandeur had shoved me a bit too forcefully out of the way in the street in his inebriated state, and I had fallen down in the snow. Daniel had locked eyes on him, and as he advanced, rather like a lion stalking his prey, the other man began to retreat, realising what a large blunder he had made. Daniel had charged after him, and within seconds they were both well out of sight. We knew nothing of his whereabouts until the following morning, when we learned that he had spent the night in a police cell in Byker, or 'the drunk tank' as it is more widely known. I had been worried sick, and Rob's calming reassurances got me through the night.

"He's probably just in the drunk tank pet, he's in a good place. I heard that they've even got double beds and luxury quilts in there now, and an à la carte menu to help the drunks sober up before they can be released back into every day society." Despite breaking the guys nose pretty badly, and also giving the poor police officer who happened to get in the way a good clout, Daniel had emerged right as rain later the next morning, saying that he had got away with a 'drunk and disorderly' caution. This was on the condition that he attended a course called 'turning point" the following month, the purpose of which, according to the letter that Daniel had brought back with him, was to 'turn your life around.' I can still remember the howls of laughter from Sally, Rob and I that morning once we read that letter.

I caught myself smiling at this memory, and quickly came back to earth as I recalled the gravity of the situation. Thankfully, after just a couple of rings, Ravindu answered.

"What on earth did you say to Daniel?"
He sounded weary, very far from his usual happy self.
"I'm so sorry. This is all my fault. What happened? What did he say to you?"
"That's the thing. He turned up just as we finished playing the gig, and then he said to come and have a

beer at the bar. And then he was just talking normally...then all of a sudden, a punch came flying out of bloody nowhere. While my head was turned the other way, he hit me right in the eye. I can't say I didn't deserve it, I suppose."

"But are you alright?"

"I've been better."

"Come here, Ravi. We'll have a drink and make it all better."

"I really don't think that's a good idea, Lilee. Daniel is probably on his way back over there now. I really don't want this to happen again in front of a different audience."

Of course, Ravindu was completely right, and the sensible voice of reason. My feelings however, didn't just cloud my judgement of reality, they extirpated it. "I'll come there then. I can't bear to think of you hurt. This is what he always does, answers to scenarios with his fists rather than his head. He's a total meathead-" I swivelled round to see curious faces turned in my direction, anxious to know what was causing me to spend so long on the telephone away from the table, probably waving my arms as though conducting an invisible orchestra as I often did whenever I got worked up. With a pang of guilt I remembered it was Audrey's birthday, and that she and Beatrice had given up their usual jaunt to Colombo to spend the weekend here instead. I hoped it wasn't a decision they were now regretting.

"Lilee? Are you alright?" Audrey had come over to the balcony, concern in her eyes.

"Urgh, what a mess this is. Don't worry, it will all sort itself out soon enough I hope. Are you having a good birthday?" I tried desperately to divert attention from the situation, but knew I wouldn't be able to do so for long. I came back to the table and downed my beer, unable to take my eyes away from my phone in case Ravindu messaged. I knew it was incredibly rude, and I was always the first to complain whenever I was at a social situation and everyone was glued to their phones.

As a golden rule, my phone was always tucked away in my bag on silent whenever I was out of the house. However tonight was an emergency. It was perhaps a good thing that I had been pinging messages back and forward as it kept me distracted from the fact that Daniel had already returned from his evening of face clobbering, and was now sitting calmly on another table with Alex grinning from ear to ear. Even though I had seen it many times, I still couldn't believe how he could just exchange his demeanour so quickly; from a rampant Tasmanian devil destroying all in his path, to a cool cucumber. It was terrifying. I couldn't just sit there and watch him pretend that nothing that happened and I grabbed my things and made to leave. Making lame excuses I stormed past Daniel who leered harshly at me, the smuggest of smirks plastered on that arrogant face I did not love. I should have continued to walk past him but I could not ignore that antagonistic sneer.

"You think you're brilliant, don't you? Because you go to the gym every day and have big muscles and can beat people up? Does it make you feel powerful? Well you might think it's attractive, but it's been your downfall tonight, because I absolutely hate it." Daniel said nothing, but he didn't have to. The gaze from his cold grey eyes cut through me like a wire. As I walked away from him for the last time, I heard the real monster escape from its human host.

"He's just an effing monkey Lilee. He can't even speak English properly man. Is it because of the poverty that you like him? Sri Lankans are fresh out of the jungle man. He'll just use you and move on to the next tourist."

I didn't give Daniel the satisfaction of turning round, yet his words rang in my ears. For once, I was putting my cards on the table, going all in instead of playing it safe like I had always done, and ending up in relationships that were just friendships and tolerances.

Chapter 11 – rice flicking

Monday November 13th
2017
Kandy, Sri Lanka

I woke up having barely slept and quickly dressed for the day. So much had happened over the weekend and it all felt like a blur, yet even to this day the events which passed remain so vivid in my mind.

I had spent the Sunday night at Subashi's house as her parents were away for the weekend, and so she had invited Alina and I round for either a 'girl's night', or probably the more likely reason was to find out what on earth this mess was that I had got myself into. My head was spinning so fast I felt like I was going to collapse, my hands shook like I was a crack addict, I couldn't breathe, and felt nauseous, all at once. I had never reacted this badly to wine, though we had drank a fair amount the previous night. My heartbeat thundered in my throat, almost with the power of a thousand galloping horses, and my saliva tasted metallic.

'What the hell's wrong with me?' I began to panic, and really really panic. I had never experienced this before. Maybe I really had overdone it and gone too far this time, and this is what liver failure symptoms were.

"You're having a panic attack. Not unexpected considered everything that's happened. Take this and breathe into it, until you feel better in a couple of minutes. Just remember what we talked about last night. Damage control."

Thrusting a paper bag over my face, Subashi's expression remained serious, and very matter of fact. I was the youngest of the three of us, but had never really acknowledged that fact until last night. I was like the terrible younger sister who constantly made erratic life decisions and then everyone else had to pick up the pieces. Subashi was right about the paper bag trick though. It really did work, and I was able to calm down relatively quickly.

"Do you both honestly think I could lose my job?" I asked again for the hundredth time. I guess I was just hoping the answer would change from the one that they had given me last night.

"If you were in Europe, or even Colombo for that matter, it wouldn't matter one bit. But this is Kandy, the most conservative and traditional town in the entire country. And this is a scandal. If this gets out amongst the parents, that you have left your English husband for a local, it will ruin your reputation and quite possibly that of the school's."

"It is actually written in my job contract, that I must not do anything that could harm the reputation of the school," I said flatly.

"So you have to go straight to Mr Ranawana, and tell him the story, before he hears it from anyone else. Even though I know you don't want to discuss your personal life with him, if someone complains about you to him first and you haven't been up front with him, you don't have a leg to stand on."

The jitters did not stop until I arrived at school, and I switched onto autopilot mode. That was, until first break, when I noticed Faiqa, the head of English, waving frantically at me in the corridor.

"I have to talk to you Lilee. Daniel has sent me some really awful messages about you." As she grabbed her phone to show me, I touched her gently on the shoulder.

"Not here, Faiqa. Let's find an empty classroom."

As we stepped inside, she showed me what Daniel had sent. Amongst the effing and blinding he had accused me of sleeping around half the local Tuk Tuk driver population and taking drugs. "Do you think someone like that should be teaching at your school?" he had written, and I could almost hear the malice in the text.

"We have to go to Mr Ranawana," whispered Faiqa, her face solemn. "If Daniel sent this to me and I only ever met him once, I have no idea who else he has sent these kinds of messages to."

"I can't thank you enough, Faiqa. Thank you so much for telling me directly, and not sharing this with the whole staffroom and revelling in the gossip."

"That's not all, Lilee. Vagina (Vijaya) is up to no good as usual too. I had Year 11 English first period, and he interrupted my lesson to ask me if he knew what had happened with you and Daniel.

He said "Don't help her out," and that he knows everything that's happened.

"Lilee doesn't know how to behave," he was saying.

Although I knew full well that I was neither innocent nor blameless in this situation, I couldn't help but feel that this was totally ridiculous. Fury spread through my nervous system like a virus. As Vagina was a relative of my landlords, Mr and Mrs Nugawela had to be behind this. Either Daniel had spoken to them directly, or they had been watching like vultures and had put two and two together. Subashi hadn't been wrong at all about how much of a scandal this was. In Newcastle no-one would have batted an eyelid. God only knows what conclusion they had come to. I wouldn't be surprised if they had spread around that I had participated in an orgy with seventeen bus drivers, eight street dogs, four monkeys, a snake and three cockroaches.

"Will you come with me?" I asked Faiqa nervously.

"Of course," she smiled, and I could see that it was an honest and caring smile, not the pretend sympathetic one you often are met with in these kinds of situations.

As Mr Ranawana read the message on Faiqa's phone, his brow furrowed as he grimaced.

"What a bloody useless fellow, trying to make trouble."

"Obviously sir, none of that is true. What is true is that we have separated, and I assume that he will be returning to the UK very soon. My concern is that we have no idea who else he has sent such poisonous messages to, and you know how some people believe everything they read. What if the parents are some of the recipients of messages such as this one?"

Mr Ranawana paused for a moment, and then waved his hand, as if flapping the situation and its unpleasantness away. I wish it was as simple as that.

"Ignore it and delete it. Don't reply, or do anything to encourage him. As for worrying what people will say, don't, because it will happen anyway. People have said things about me for the past 50 years, I don't care. Just keep doing what you're doing, coming into school and doing a good job."

"Will this issue affect my contract, or my ability to stay here sir?" The thought of having to leave the school where I had found my passionate and enthusiastic teacher self again was almost painful.

"Not at all. Just keep doing what you're doing, and keep your head held high. It will blow over. We are with you." I breathed a sigh of heavy relief, unable to quite believe my luck at how calmly he had perceived this situation. As we thanked Mr Ranawana and turned to leave his office, he finished with the exact reasoning that Ravindu had said over the weekend in an attempt to make me feel a bit better.

"In the war, Prabhakaran, the leader of the Tamil tigers, did say one true thing about Sinhalese people. They talk and talk and all, yet they forget everything in a couple of weeks."

"Let's hope it's true!" I almost laughed with hysteria.

As we walked back through to the staffroom, we passed Mr Ranawana's personal assistant, Imodini, who Malcolm used to refer to as the diarrhoea relief medicine 'Immodium' owing to the permanently unpleasant look on her face. She loved gossip, and I glowered at her as I noticed her smirking with glee as though what she had clearly overheard in Mr Ranawana's office was as pleasurable as her most recent bowel movement.

By the end of the day, I felt much better. My Year 8 German class had been brilliant and fun to teach as always. I had had the same students the previous year, and I honestly felt that they enjoyed their time in lessons with me as much as I did them. It was very strange and unique how I had bonded with that year group, and it hadn't happened before. As I signed out at two, I checked my phone for the first time that day. My reaction to the messages I had from Alex prompted a couple of teachers to ask me if everything was alright.

"Yeah – fine thanks. See you all tomorrow!" I ran as fast as I possibly could outside, desperately hoping that my driver wouldn't be late. Thankfully, he was there on time.
"Where do you want to go Madam?"
"Commercial bank please. I know there's school traffic, but if you can get there in ten minutes, I'll pay you double!"
"Ok Madam, we go this way. Other way fuuuuull block!"

I rushed into the bank as fast as my short legs would carry me. I had the internet banking app on my phone, but did not dare look at it, though I already knew that Alex's warnings had been far from a false alarm. I should have shut the account down much earlier, though I never thought that Daniel would stoop this low. I now just needed to complete damage control: level 2.
"The problem is Madam; it is a joint account, so we cannot close it without the signatures of both you and

your husband."

"Ok. Can I open a different account now then in my name only, and transfer whatever is left in the other account over?"

The assistant fiddled with his keyboard, scrolled and clicked the mouse a few times, as banking people generally do. He frowned slightly.

"Madam, there is nothing in this account. Well, except 56 rupees."

All the feeling drained from my face. 54 rupees was about 30 pence. This morning there had been about a million rupees in there, about four and a half thousand pounds. Everything I had managed to save despite Daniel drinking so much away. Ok, so around a quarter of it was what Daniel had earned in Germany over the summer, and was what I expected that he would have taken when I had read the frantic warning messages from Alex that Daniel was leaving for the airport, saying he was going to 'clean me out.'

I took a deep breath, trying to regain composure considering that I was in the middle of the bank, in the middle of town, and there were many eyes on me.

"Ok. You seem like a clever man, and I'm sure you can work out what's happened. Can I please open another account in my name only?"

"Ayyoooo, Madam, I'm afraid foreigners can only have one bank account."

"Can I see that rule in writing please?"

This was usually the trick here to get what you wanted, and failing that, hand over some cash. Salaries were so low that bribery was an everyday occurrence; particularly the police. For small things like parking misdemeanours, or being caught doing something silly when drunk, the whole paying off thing worked brilliantly, though for more serious offences like drink driving, it was really bad. The assistant shifted uncomfortably in his seat, and mumbled that he would go and speak to the manager. It only took a few minutes and he was back, delicately placing a pen and paper in front of me.

"Ok Madam. You write request letter to manager asking if we can open new account, and we will do it. Just for you, ok?" He smiled broadly, and I knew that he comprehended the situation fully. I wondered if he had been the one who had handed over everything to Daniel earlier that day; there's no way he could have withdrawn all that at a cashpoint. I consoled myself that phrase two of damage control was complete, and tried not to think about what on earth I would do until payday in almost two weeks' time.

Friday 12th January 2018
Kandy, Sri Lanka

After a couple of weeks back again to the UK for Christmas and New Year, which was an unavoidable trip simply for the fact I a) had to explain myself to everyone and (b) reassure everyone that I was ok, I landed back in

Sri Lanka with a suitcase packed full of Christmas cake, Christmas pudding, and mince pies for the staff at school to try. Unfortunately what I had failed to realise was that all contained some form of alcohol, usually a brandy of some sort.

In my religious ignorance; probably a result of paying little to no attention in religious education lessons at school, I had thought that the presence of alcohol in food was no problem at all, and so had said nothing as I served up the yummy treats in the staffroom. Naturally, the teachers had excitedly flocked to the table, grabbing whatever they could. It was the biggest display of human greed I had ever seen in my life; some were swatting each other away and flapping like seagulls in the race to get to the plate first and get the biggest portion. It was only when Ranjan, the deputy head started waving his hand frantically in front of his mouth that the others began to realise that there was alcohol inside.

"Is there alcohol in this?!" asked Faiqa, shock in her eyes.

"I'm so sorry; I honestly thought if it was in food it didn't matter. Like I thought you just didn't drink a glass of something alcoholic. I'm honestly really sorry, it's not one of those things I've ever clarified really, and I suppose I should have done." I repeated the same poor excuse over and over again, and luckily all but about three staff members thought it was hilarious.

"I'm going to be teaching my lesson drunk! Ayyoooo! I'll

have to get some mints. I hope the students don't smell it on my breath!" Piumi the maths teacher chuckled merrily.

Despite feeling a little bad that I had probably condemned half the staff to eternal punishment in their religious beliefs, I couldn't help but feel that I was much more tolerant of their eating habits. I came to actively dread the time where people would begin to snap open their lunchboxes, for the stench of *Maldives fish* would infiltrate my nostrils faster than the dosage of the lethal injection enters the veins of a prisoner on death row. Once, one of the maths teachers who I was unfortunate enough to sit next to in the staffroom had been eating his lunch of rice and curry by hand, as is the normal way in most south Asian countries. I didn't have a problem with that at all of course – but I did feel slightly outraged when he flicked his hand, sending grains of sticky rice splattering onto my cheek, into my hair, and even one went in my eye. He was totally oblivious to his etiquette abomination, and simply stood up, snorted, and walked away.
"mmmm, lecker!" said Belinda, the other German teacher in the department. (Lecker means tasty in German). From that day on, this poor unsuspecting teacher was known as 'lecker.'

At this point, Ravindu and I were still being extremely careful who saw us together and where we met, as it was still only six or seven weeks following Daniel's departure. It was way too soon to risk the flare up of gossip again. This said, our meeting place would usually be Slightly Chilled on a Friday night, and the concoction of flowing drinks and strong feelings only ever led to one outcome. I had missed him terribly over the Christmas holidays, and whether my eyes were open or closed, I found it difficult to see anything other than his face. With his vast mane of luscious curls, he was like a lion. Even without Daniel in the equation, we would still have our fair share of challenges; physical displays of affection in Asian countries in general are extremely looked down on, particularly in India and Sri Lanka.

When my mum and brother had been over to visit in the October, I had taken them to the Peradeniya botanical gardens, which are beautifully maintained, but all of the trees and vegetation make for the ultimate hideaway for couples escaping from the wrath and judgement of their parents and the community. I felt so sorry for them when observing the security guards storming around the park, blasting their whistle at couples simply for holding hands.

"Podi lamai innewa! Discipline danne ne!" (small children are here! You don't know discipline!) They barked. Part of me found this hilarious, and the other part of me felt really sad that it was so bad to show affection or love for someone. I couldn't imagine what these security guards would make of the parties I had attended on Friday nights at the ice rink. You could often only get a glimpse of a side profile, as there were so many tongues down throats. I remember marvelling at beautiful girls in figure skates, and the scruffy bad boys in ice hockey skates, holding hands and skating around each other. The youth here had none of that excitement, none of that romance.

On a second thought, I suppose romance exists everywhere in the world, just in different ways. Once coming out of my memory of Peradeniya gardens, I glanced down at my phone to see an array of messages and missed calls from Alina. Puzzled, I phoned her back. She answered after just one ring.
"Can I come over? For like a few days? I'm sorry, I didn't know who else to call." The only thing that sounded similar was her unmistakable Slavic-American accent.
"Of course you can! I'll stick the kettle on and have a tea ready." This was one British saying that I did believe in; that all problems can be solved by a cup of tea. I mused for a few moments, wondering what the issue could be.

When Alina arrived, she didn't just have an overnight bag with her. She had a large backpack and two other big bags with her. I said nothing of course, and gave my friend a big hug.
"I'll get the tea. You sit and chill for a few minutes, and then you can get whatever it is off your chest, if you want to." I began to wonder if she had split up with Sanjit, her husband. Her eyes were red and puffy as though she'd been crying.

"So, what's brought this on then?" I asked lightly, hoping that whatever damage had been done was reversible.

"I just can't live there anymore. I really can't. I've managed it for a year. But it's too much."

Alina and Sanjit had previously shared an apartment together when they lived and worked in Colombo, however when they had decided to set up their tourism business they moved in with Sanjit's parents in the outskirts of Kandy for the location and financial practicalities. It had been no secret that Alina had become unhappy there; I think any wife would find living with their in-laws difficult to tolerate. I know I could only manage a maximum of two days staying with Daniel's family. I felt bad for the amount of times I had whinged to Alina about them; how insensitive of me.

Not unlike how it must have been in the 1950's and earlier in Europe, in Sri Lanka it is still an expectation and often a necessity for the wife to move into the parental home of the husband, and help to cook and care for his parents in their older age. Although one of Alina's favourite things to do was to cook, she had found the complete lack of personal space and breach of privacy too much to bear. Sanjit's mum would burst into her room at 4 in the morning and insist that she wake up, take food that Alina had brought from Slovenia from the fridge, try and fail to cook it, and throw it in the bin. I was very surprised that she had been able to put up with this for so long, and it appeared that the feuds between Alina and her mother in law were now causing arguments and friction between Alina and Sanjit themselves.

In the end, 'a few days' became six months. I didn't mind this at all and greatly welcomed the company as well as being able to share out the cooking. Having Alina there helped with my defences against Mr and Mrs Nugawela somewhat; whose level of interference had gone into overdrive once they learned that Daniel had left. They did not understand nor welcome the concept of a female living alone, and so they relaxed a bit once Alina had moved in. They had however hinted that we should pay more rent, which was ludicrous as there had been Daniel as well as myself staying there previously and Sanjit was only there occasionally, so there was little difference, if any.

Chapter 12 – Sorry madam, sad mood

Monday 5th March 2018
Kandy, Sri Lanka

By March, almost four months had passed, and Ravindu was now staying over. As we often had friends around for dinner, and Sanjit was coming and going through the night, it was less possible for Mrs and Mrs Nugawela to 'police' who came in and out of the house. They did not comprehend the role of a landlord at all; that as long as you pay the rent on time and in full, which I did without fail, they had little other reason to be involved in our lives. By now I had had enough of tip toeing around them, and worrying what more tales they would tell Vagina about me. Having Alina there gave me the confidence to reassert myself.

I got a bit of a shock at school that morning, and for once it wasn't Mr and Mrs Nugawela or Vagina who were responsible. It was a message from Ravindu with a surprise revelation.
"My aunt has found someone for me to marry in Colombo. A teacher as well apparently! Can you believe it?"
Although I was sitting at my desk in the staffroom, my mouth fell open, appalled. I caught myself quickly, hoping that others didn't notice. I actually couldn't believe it; it actually felt like I had been shot, and was completely winded, unable to breathe. I shoved my phone back into my bag, and went to do my register. I had nothing to say back to him. It is an unwritten rule in relationships that if they read the message but don't reply, you're in the danger zone.

Four fabulous lessons later, I felt that my strength was restored enough to confront Ravi at the end of the school day. He had interpreted my reading and not replying well, and clearly knew he was in the danger zone.
"Babu? Are you mad?"
I began to type furiously.
"Of course I'm not exactly happy at the fact you're bloody getting married! Was this all just a bit of fun for you? I can't believe I took such a risk for you and how I

got it all so wrong! Good luck with her I'm sure she'll be just perfect."

Ravi rang straight away. I was tempted to reject the call, as his voice was so smooth so I knew upon hearing it I would cave in to whatever excuses he was going to give. Curiosity got the better of me however and I answered.
"Whoa babu, easy easy! I never said anything about getting married! My aunt can't make me do anything. I have no intention of getting married, not to anyone except you!"
"Well, you sounded excited and happy about the idea. And she'll never accept me anyway, seeing as I'm the wrong colour, a *suddi,* right? So maybe in the long term this is best for you anyway."
Ravi paused for a moment before speaking again.
"You have to see it from her side. She just thinks I'm rattling around that house on my own and lonely, with no-one to cook for me or any company. It's her way of trying to help," explained Ravindu lightly.
"So you're definitely not getting married?"
Ravi burst out laughing.
"Honestly Lilee, you're so funny sometimes. Of course not. I've been there done that before. Trust me, I could never go back to being with someone who doesn't want to do anything, not even go for a walk or a swim!"

I arrived home to raucous laughter, as Ravindu had clearly shared our conversation with Alina. I was sure that she enjoyed our misunderstandings. Although there was not an issue with a language barrier as such, there were certain things that Ravi said which in Europe you would just never say, and often I would take in a way that he didn't expect. Having been in Sri Lanka for many more years than I, Alina was much more experienced at dealing with these kind of situations.

One example was today when he went into a dangerous new territory where no man should ever go. The domain of weight. Ravindu had tried a quiche for the first time ever yesterday, and there was enough left over for our lunch today. Unfortunately he had decided to insult the chef rather than compliment.
"You're just like a quiche!" Ravi grinned, his eyes bouncing happily.
"Cheesy, but with juuuust the right amount of fat."
"*Fat!?* Alina, he thinks I'm fat. Right, that's it. I'm going on hunger strike!"
"I'm sure he means it as a good thing, said Alina, smirking. "Here, being fat means wealth and prosperity. That's why the saris are worn the way they are, with the blouse pushing down on the love handles so they splurge out!"
"Exactly!" chirped Ravi. "Why would any guy want a girl who looks as flat as a bloody *Carrom* board?"

By now, I had learned just how much Sri Lankans loved cricket of course, but also the game of '*Carrom*' as well. Many young men could often be seen in their homes, furiously flicking the wooden counters into the corners of the square board, whilst drinking *arrack,* or Johnnie Walker Black Label Whiskey if they were more affluent. "Stop body shaming women!" I uttered indignantly. "No wonder so many of us have self-esteem issues, with people like you!"

Ravi was clearly thrilled that for once, today Alina had defended him. It was a rarity. Although there hadn't been any ructions at all in the house, there had been a couple of small clashes between Alina and Ravindu, usually in the kitchen. One example was when Alina had asked Ravindu to grab some chicken from the market, and he had returned not with a healthy pink breast, but what looked more like a pair of greying smoker's lungs. "We can't seriously use that!" Alina and I had doubled over in fits of laughter.
"There's nothing wrong with it!" Ravi had retorted, his eyes glimmering with hurt and disappointment.

A similar culinary argument had erupted when Ravi had made *pol sambol* using the usual ingredients; scraped coconut, lime, onions, and chillies, though he had used green ones which had displeased Alina intensely.
"You are supposed to use red ones!" she had complained, her words spiking his fragile pride like barbed wire.
"Who's the Sri Lankan one, huh?" he riposted, raising an eyebrow.

Suddenly Alina's phone rang. As soon as she answered, her face changed completely from the smiling expression she had worn just moments earlier. I instinctively knew something was wrong as the pitch of her voice ascended rapidly with anxiety as she spoke with her husband.

"Riots have broken out in Digana. Sanjit can't get anywhere, for they've put a big army road block in place. Loads of Muslim owned shops have been burned down, and some people have been attacked and even killed."

I couldn't believe what I was hearing. The three of us stared at each other in shock for a whole minute. I refused to believe, I would not believe, that this had happened just half an hour away from our home where I had always felt so safe and at peace.

My thoughts turned to my students, and I tried to stop horror from seeping into my mind, though this was difficult. There were a lot of Muslim students at Thambili International School. Were any of them affected, or worse, hurt?

All but two of my sweet Year 8 class who tried so hard every lesson and were so talented were Muslims who lived in the area. I hoped and prayed that they were all alright, and I assumed that I would see them at school the following day as normal.

Soon however, it was announced on the news that a curfew had been imposed that night. One night turned into two nights, and then two nights turned into a week. Schools were closed. Supermarkets emptied as people panic bought. The waiting and suspense was the worst, not knowing whether the tensions would calm down or escalate. President Sirisena declared a state of emergency. Facebook and all other social media was blocked so to stop the spread of hate speech. What the authorities did not realise was that most people simply downloaded VPN's to get around this obstacle.

Finally, after a week of limbo, we returned to school. Routines resumed. Tensions faded, but were not forgotten. As I arrived at school on the first day back, I felt apprehensive. As it was a mixed school, how would the students behave with one another?

Wednesday 28th March 2018
Kandy, Sri Lanka

It was only three weeks after the unrest close to Kandy which had made international news, though I was really glad that one of my best friends, Bella, had still decided to make the trip over to visit for a couple of weeks. Her arrival coincided with that of Kasun who was one of Ravi's best friends who was living and working abroad in Kuwait. On Wednesday evenings Ravi played at the Ganga Addara hotel, and Bella and I had decided to go along and watch the band play and meet Kasun as he would be staying with us until Sunday.

Ganga Addara had a lot of potential to be a fantastic venue, however as usual it was completely dead.

Nevertheless, we decided to liven the place up ourselves, knocking back a few drinks. I hadn't realised how much lower my tolerance level had gone until I figured that I could no longer keep up with Bella. She had only been here since Sunday but we'd had so many laughs already. The driver from the airport had been particularly grumpy, and was rather rotund in shape. He drove a 'Tata Nano' car, which I described as a semi-circle.

"Well that was a full circle alright, with his belly. He completed the full round!"

Bella gestured with her hands and we both fell about laughing. I'd never look at those abysmal cars in the same way again.

Tonight proved to be no different. Thankfully the gins hit us fairly quickly, and we were laughing and chatting away with Kasun who was very easy going and friendly. I had been a bit apprehensive about meeting him as I knew that he had also known Ravindu's ex-wife.

"Were you friends with her? Ravi's ex-wife?" I blurted out, emboldened by the gin.

"Bloody hell, Lilee! That's no way to introduce yourself to someone!" Bella burst out laughing as I rubbed my cheeks, realising my mistake. Kasun smiled kindly.

"Don't worry man, its fine. Yeah I was friends with her, but haven't spoken to her since you know..." He trailed off and we all turned our heads, for someone else had taken the stage.

The singer, clearly very confident, belted out a song from the depth of his large lungs. He swung his arms out with the force of a rugby player as he performed, making us all sit bolt upright to attention.

"He reminds me of love lace. You know that penguin from happy feet with the really deep voice? I think it's the hair." Bella said. We both exploded in fits of giggles, which were even more uncontrollable when the singer suddenly swung his arm forward with such power he lost his balance, crashing into a speaker which was then consequently knocked over. It was one of the funniest sights ever.

The next day, we decided to take the bus to Sigiriya rock, named by some as the 'eighth wonder of the world.' I had taken the Thursday and Friday off work in order to make a long weekend so I could travel a bit with Bella. Thambili International was fantastic in this way; each member of staff was entitled to three days paid personal leave per term on top of the holidays we already had. It is common knowledge that teachers get the best holidays, though nobody realises that they are set in stone, which means that we cannot take holidays when we actually need them. This system allowed us so much flexibility for which I am still extremely grateful. No such thing exists in the UK. I remember requesting to take a day off to accompany Daniel to his grandmother's funeral, and the request was denied on the basis that it was not direct family.

I had taken the bus previously many times in Sri Lanka, and I had already taken this particular route three times without any issue. However today was different.

As the driver veered around the bends at such speed the suspension was bent over at almost a 45 degree angle, I became aware of a man pressing his manhood a little too hard into my shoulder. In these kinds of situations, you have to be 100% sure it's not just the movement of the bus before you confront, which can be quite hard to determine. I decided to activate the selfie camera on my phone to double check I wasn't overreacting, and watched him as he made a small clockwise gyration which was definitely not caused by the movement of the bus. 'Gotcha', I thought as I took photos. I held the camera there a little longer until the dirty bastard looked down and clocked what I was doing. He practically ran down to the other end of the bus as I looked up at him and stared him straight in the eye and called him a *val minihek* which translates roughly to 'pervert' in Sinhala.

This was only the first undesirable encounter of the day. We made it to Sigiriya unscathed, Bella especially as I had made sure that she sat next to the window. We enjoyed the view at the top of Pidurangala rock with its adjacent view of Sigiriya which is absolutely breath-taking. As much as we would have loved to stay and watch the sun set, we decided to catch a bus back before night fell and more extremely sexually frustrated men would be out to partake on their regular night of passenger groping rituals. As we negotiated with a Tuk Tuk driver to take us from the rock to the bus stop, he began trying to overcharge us.

"I know how far it is. I've been here many times," I said wearily in Sinhala. Although my salary was tax free, as most international school salaries are, I still had to pay a "skin tax" almost everywhere I went.

"Madam, look my phone. I show you Google map."

I took his phone and began to type the location of the bus stop, but fell about laughing when his search history brought up 'Indian sex'. I showed Bella and we were howling with laughter. Realising his fatal mistake, the driver reached desperately for his phone.

"My brother searching, madam," he said. I could feel his absolute mortification, knowing that we would never forget this moment and that would be how we would forever remember him. He dropped us before the bus stop, advising us that we were more likely to get a seat before everyone else got on at the central bus stand. I figured that he was desperately trying to recover from the amount of face he had lost.

As we sat close to the front of the bus, it was only about 15 minutes before darkness fell, and my prediction came true. As Bella closed her eyes for a quick nap, I noticed that a younger guy was jerking his leg every so often with the movement of the bus, touching her leg. He then proceeded to go further rubbing his leg up and down hers. He had gone too far.

"What are you doing?!" I yelled, causing everyone to

stare at the man. As with anything that involves embarrassment or 'losing face' as they say in Asia, the man was taken aback and mortified.

"I'm very sorry madam," he said.

"You're not sorry, or you wouldn't bloody do it!"

By now Bella was wide awake and aware of what was happening.

"What happened Lilee? Did he touch me? Urgh, dirty bastard!"

The man was now unsure of what to do, as the weight of two northern English girls threatened to crush him and any ounce of dignity he had.

"Madam, I am sorry. Sad mood," said the man. He was dressed up in a smart flannel shirt, and I wondered if he had been fired from his job, or rejected by a woman. No surprise at all if the latter were the reason for his unhappy state.

"Sad mood? Is that seriously a reason?!" Bella and I choked up laughing. The man was now so embarrassed he got off the bus at the earliest opportunity, probably preferring to wait for the next bus so he could chance his luck with someone else.

I thought that my outburst would have done the trick to ward off any more predators, but unfortunately not. Two men got on the bus, and it was clear that they had been drinking. One was dressed in a smart black shirt, and the other in a rugby top.

"They look a bit more sophisticated," said Bella, unknowingly tempting fate. Rugby top stared at us as though we were delicious ice creams, and did not take his eyes off us even when I asked him not to stare in Sinhala. Unfortunately, this had the completely opposite effect to what I had hoped for.

"Madam, you know Sinhala?" leered black shirt, his tongue almost hanging out of his mouth like a hungry dog.

"A bit."

"You married? Husband? You like Sri Lankan boys eh?"

What I had learned from this experience was that in future, it was better to never open a dialogue, especially if the offender was not alone. Direct confrontation usually worked, as I recall one time I stupidly decided to catch the last bus from Colombo to Kandy. Halfway through the journey, I realised that the man sitting next to me with his arms folded was in fact stroking the side of my breast with his right hand, which was cleverly folded under his left arm as a disguise. As soon as I yelled,

"What are you doing?" accompanied by one or two expletives of course, the pervert politely whispered,

"I'm very sorry madam," and getting off the bus at the earliest possible opportunity as a forest of eyes stared.

There are several factors which result in this type of unchallenged behaviour, particularly on public transport. One of the main reasons for this is the government school system. Unlike international schools, which are mixed like the majority of schools are in Europe, many government schools are segregated by gender and religion. Therefore, you have Buddhist boy's schools, Buddhist girl's schools, Islamic boy's schools, and Islamic girl's schools, Hindu boy's schools and Hindu girl's schools and so on. The first colossal problem with this is once the students leave school and enter society, they have no idea how to interact with other young people who are the opposite sex, or from a different religious background. The term 'divide and conquer' springs to mind.

The second problem is that culturally, any reference to sex whatsoever is considered highly 'taboo,' and so there is no sexual health education or testing in schools. Despite Ravindu's open mindedness and eagerness to learn about other countries and cultures, he too is a product of the government school system, and at age 31 knew little about sexually transmitted diseases or how to get tested. I understand that it is incorrect to say that western culture is right, and other cultures are wrong, but when it gets to such a point that people's health and safety is compromised in order to 'protect the culture', one has to argue that there's something amiss.

Following our traumatic trip to Sigiriya, we decided to head to Nuwara Eliya up in the mountains for a couple of days, and Ravi and Kasun decided that they would meet us there as we wouldn't be able to leave until the late afternoon once I had finished work. Bella panicked slightly as we waded through the crowds at the dusty

Kandy bus station, as bus conductors hollered their destinations at the top of their lungs, as if one might change their mind about where they were travelling to depending on the strength of the conductor's voice. We found our bus, as the conductor made eye contact and bellowed at us. "Nuwara-nuwara-nuwara-eliyaaaaaaaaa!"

"What's he saying?" whimpered Bella. "He sounds really angry?"

"Maybe the CD with his favourite bus music has broken or maybe he's had a fight with the driver because he forgot to hang the lime and chillies under the bus," I mused thoughtfully. We were interrupted by more hollering, this time from a man walking up and down the bus selling round deep fried and delicious lentil snacks called *vade* (pronounced like vaday).

"vade vade vade vadeeeee. Vade vade isso vade..."

"No chance of having a nap on these is there?" said Bella, as she bought some vade to try.

We arrived in Nuwara Eliya to wonderfully welcoming cool and fresh air and a street dog, balefully looking up at us. Bella tossed him some vade that was left over from our journey, but he slid it aside with his paw, and refused to touch it.

"How ungrateful!" tutted Bella. Ravi and Kasun suggested that we meet in a local restaurant for dinner, and hungry from our three hour journey up slow and winding roads, we were happy to oblige.

The restaurant was teeming with people tucking into *dosai, idli, rotti,* and *string hoppers,* and the curries on each table were as full of colour as an abstract painting, the kind where the artist takes bright colours and throws them everywhere. We took our seats, ready to fill our faces. Ravi mixed rice and three different curries, and made it into a ball with his hand as he ate. Without warning, he swiftly scooped his hand with the rice ball he had just squished together towards my mouth, and I recoiled in terror.

"What on earth are you doing?!"

"Feeding you."

Bella and I looked at each other before bursting into awkward laughter.

"We don't need to be fed by someone else after the age of three!" I noticed to my consternation that Ravindu looked a little upset and rejected.

"It's showing you I care. Feeding each other is a very caring and nice thing to do. My cousins love my mixings."

Culturally, the whole feeding thing is probably one of the biggest differences. In western cultures, the idea of someone feeding you as a teenager or adult is hugely embarrassing and outright weird. Even eating from the hand is only really commonplace for things like sandwiches or pizza, definitely not rice and curry. One friend who came to visit me really couldn't handle having no fork and knife, so she improvised by using her bank card to scoop up the rice and curry!

However in Sri Lanka, feeding others is very important and it brings great happiness to the person who feeds you. For instance, seventy year old mothers will even still feed their fifty year old sons at the dinner table with rice and curry from their hand.

"Ok, I'll give it a try. But not in front of all these people, where I'll probably freak out and drop it all down myself. We can practice first at home if it makes you happy."
Ravi smiled.
"Yes. Let's find a middle ground." The 'middle ground' was Ravi's favourite and most commonly used expression.

The two weeks that Bella spent with us passed in a flash, and it had been such a breath of fresh air to have her come and stay. As Sri Lankan women don't go out at all (with Subashi being the only exception) admittedly my social life in Kandy was pretty restricted, and Bella's visit had been a laugh a day, which had been just what I needed.

Chapter 13 – Freckly deer

Friday, 13th April 2018
Trincomalee, Sri Lanka

The Easter holidays or the Sinhala & Tamil New Year holidays I should say, arrived in the blink of an eye, and Subashi and I had organised a 10 day trip away as we all had the fortnight off work. On the first day, we had travelled to Habarana to go on a safari, where we had seen a whole herd of elephants at Kaudulla national park, bathing in the water hole. There were so many babies, though sadly also so many jeeps packed with tourists and locals alike. The next stage of our holiday took us to Trincomalee, which offered the popular beach resorts of Uppaveli and Nilaveli on the north eastern coast of the island. After spending a couple of days here, we would bus it down to Arugam Bay, on the south eastern coast.

Today marked the last day of the Sinhala & Tamil year, and the New Year would dawn at 8.13 in the morning the following day, on the 14th April 2018. The time of the New Year changes every year and is calculated using the constellations in order to generate the correct 'auspicious time.' In keeping with the New Year tradition, families boil milk rice at the correct time, and when it overflows, the direction of the overflow will indicate some prediction about the New Year to come. In addition, it is a must that people eat at a certain time, and wear a certain colour, facing in a particular direction. In 2018, the time to eat was at 10.40 in the morning, the colour to wear was blue, and the direction that they should face was north. I found it fascinating.

I had always enjoyed our New Year celebrations on December 31st, when my grandma would prepare an amazing buffet and as children we would delight in seeing all of the adults, who were normally so keen to discipline us, let their hair down and go wild. We would kick granddad out of the house just before midnight so he could be the 'first-footer' - as custom dictates, he was to walk around the block and bring in a small gift of prosperity for the New Year. He was always supposed to bring a small whisky, which grandma would hide in a different pocket each year in the hope that it would remain unopened once he returned, though unfortunately her attempts were always unsuccessful. Poor granddad, already a fair few drinks in ready to see in the New Year and to protect from the icy cold outside, could not resist the stuff. When he returned at a few minutes past midnight, grandma would start to scold him for drinking the whisky, and he would distract her by grabbing everyone together to sing Auld Lang Syne, and sooner or later someone inebriated would fall to the floor, cackling hysterically. The best New Year celebration had been the arrival of the year 2000 when everyone was convinced by the media that 'the millennium bug' would bring all technological advances to a grinding halt. In the face of such adversity, everyone partied harder than ever.

The following morning, I decided to call Mr and Mrs Nugawela and wish them well for the New Year. Although we had had our differences, it was surely the right thing to do. Mrs Nugawela answered after a few rings.
"Hello, just calling to wish you a very Happy New Year!" I tried to sound upbeat and enthusiastic despite really not being a morning person. I was not prepared for her

reply.

"Yes...happy new year to you. We are not celebrating, as my mother has just died."

Oh no. What on earth can I say? I thought. Talk about putting my foot in it. Though there was no way of knowing, especially being so far away in Trincomalee. Her mother had been ill for a considerable amount of time, and it was no surprise really – she was 97 years old.

"I'm so sorry," I replied soberly.

"If there's anything I can do...I'm going to renew my contract so I will be around to stay another year if that's ok? I can help you out with shopping and stuff."

I wasn't at all prepared for what came next.

"Actually, my daughter is going to come back from Colombo and live in the apartment. I was trying to find the right time to tell you."

I knew straight away that this was a complete lie, especially as whenever her daughter visited, she stayed in the upstairs apartment which was still vacant. Given the circumstances of her mother's death, I probably should not have pushed for the truth, but I was outraged by this lame excuse and so decided to anyway.

"But what about the upstairs apartment? Isn't that where she always stays anyway? Plus it's bigger. Doesn't it make sense for her to stay there? Just tell me the real reason, and I'll make the necessary arrangements to find somewhere else to live."

I was sure that I heard a sharp intake of breath on the other end of the line.

"You have disgraced the reputation of this family, by bringing that boy into our house when there is still a possibility that Daniel may return! You are his wife! This is a scandal. And we will not allow our name to be shamed. Please make the necessary arrangements and leave."

I knew that conflict was the last thing that Mrs Nugawela would want right now, but I couldn't hold back.

"My personal life, who I invite to the house and the situation with Daniel, which by the way - is no business of yours! You are a landlord. Your role is to collect the rent and make any necessary repairs, which haven't happened by the way."

When I mentioned the poor maintenance, I was referring to the shower in the bathroom. I was sure that a street dog could urinate with more pressure than the measly drips which feebly descended from the showerhead. I had been asking Mr and Mrs Nugawela to rectify this since I had moved in, yet had been met with the same response every time. A blank face, an "aaaaaah," and that was the end of it. There wasn't even a ceiling fan! They were simply taking all of the rent money and investing none of it back into the house, which unfortunately is often the case with landlords.

Mrs Nugawela was certainly not used to being spoken to like this, and certainly not today of all days. I did feel slightly bad, but she had no right whatsoever to judge other people and their lives, that were not hers. I was seething.

"Please make the arrangements and go."

"You call yourself a Buddhist? I thought Buddhists weren't meant to judge?"
Click. Knowing that she would never succeed in winning this argument, and clearly embarrassed at the way her prepared lie had backfired, Mrs Nugawela had hung up the phone, showing how cowardly she was. I relayed the conversation to Subashi, who was sitting on the bed, eyes wide open.

I tried not to let the unfolding situation affect the rest of the holiday, though the realisation that I was on the other side of the world and about to be evicted never left my mind. I itched to get back to Kandy so that I could get out of that house pronto.

Thursday 10th May, 2018
Kandy, Sri Lanka

After abruptly learning that I was no longer welcome, I began to search for somewhere else to live as soon as I returned to Kandy. Mr and Mrs Nugawela had made it clear that due to my change of partner, they had 'lost face', a concept that seems to exist only in Asia, and is therefore very difficult for a European to understand the severe consequences of 'losing face'. I had had a rude awakening. The most worrying aspect of their behaviour was that vile rumours about me had begun to circulate around the staffroom at school, meaning that false information was being leaked to Vijaya and his wife, who were the only possible connection between Mr and Mrs Nugawela and my school.

Such rumours were that I was throwing wild parties every night, that I was having illicit relations with several Tuk Tuk drivers, and that I didn't know how to behave. None of these of course were true, but it was clearly having Ravindu over that was causing such displeasure. Apart from that, I would often have friends over for dinner which was a reality very far from 'wild parties'. I had confronted Mrs Nugawela once getting to know of this horrid gossip that she was generating, which she of course flatly denied. The expression on her face was unmistakable and was all I needed to see to know the truth.

"Please, don't tell Vijaya anything about my personal life again," I insisted firmly.
"It has absolutely nothing to do with him, and he has no right bringing it into school. It's very unprofessional."
I could see with some satisfaction that Mrs Nugawela had clearly been caught off guard and she began to look very uncomfortable. As the head teacher of Waraka

international school, my friend Alina had mentioned that she was certainly not used to being challenged or spoken to directly and was more accustomed to being worshipped by her staff and students. Her word was usually law.

"I have never said anything," she said slowly, dark shadows dancing across the sullen expression on her face.

"Well, Vijaya must be making some very nasty things up all by himself then, as people have told me what he's been going around saying," I retorted defiantly, my blood heated.

Mrs Nugawela didn't reply and simply glowered before making her excuses and leaving.

That week I hunted desperately for somewhere to live where the landlords were as far away as possible so that there would be no risk of interfering storytellers. Unfortunately in Kandy it was generally very hard to find somewhere to rent that was a landlord free zone and for many, the concept of privacy was completely alien. Everybody knew everybody's business, to the point where nobody really needed any security cameras for they were already installed in the form of the neighbours and landlords. I looked at one place which would have been perfect however the landlords lived directly above the apartment. When I told them that Ravindu would also be staying there a few nights a week, they looked at each other in horror before reiterating what they had said from the beginning, that they were only happy to rent to foreigners. No Sri Lankans allowed.

After six similar instances I was beginning to give up. I could not understand how there could be so many who were racist to their own people. Usually renting a house was very simple in the way that you simply paid the rent on time by bank transfer and that was it. The landlord never knew nor cared who stayed in the property as long as it was not being sublet. My loyal and helpful driver Gavesh informed me that there was a twelve bedroom house just five minutes down the road from where I had been living. I shook my head vigorously as the thought of cleaning all that flooded my mind with sheer terror.

"Let's go and see," said Gavesh. "Maybe he doesn't want to give all 12 bedrooms." He did have a point. Although often looked down on in society, Tuk Tuk drivers are in many cases the wisest of them all. They know everything and everyone. I decided to bring Alina and Ravi with me so that they could help with the decision making and check that I wasn't about to go from the frying pan into the fire.

I fell in love with the house as soon as I saw it. It was a gorgeous white washed building with a Japanese style roof and a beautifully wooden carved screen inside. There was a large balcony which offered a stunning view of the knuckles mountain range which enveloped the city of Kandy, and three bedrooms on the first floor, one of which was located separately at the other side of the balcony, offering the highest degree of privacy. The wooden doors were fitted with multi-coloured glass panes, and the floors were tiled with a marble effect. The ground floor also offered a bedroom aside from a lounge area, though this was used as a study. There were two more apartments built behind the main house, each offering four rooms. It all felt too good to be true. I wondered if the landlord would be the catch, or the neighbours.

Samantha the landlord was a bizarre man, though I could tell that deep down his heart was in the right place. He had business in Japan and Italy and so travelled there frequently. He spoke at a thousand miles an hour, and as he spoke no English at all, with my basic knowledge of Sinhala I stood no chance. He was quite tall, with very thick glasses, and a slight *bundy* (belly). He waved his hands energetically as he spoke to Ravindu who he seemed to have taken a real liking to. In the typical friendly and familiar Sri Lankan way Samantha addressed Ravindu as *Malli* (younger brother).

"Malli, I don't even need the money malli. I built a new house and want someone just to keep this place clean and maintain it. I have so much money malli, do you want to see?" Samantha put his arm around Ravindu and pulled out a flurry of bank statements. "Look, malli. This one, forty lakhs. This one, two hundred lakhs. This one, one hundred and eighty lakhs.

I don't need money malli. I just want this place to stay clean."
I had never in my life seen anyone boast so much about their income, and stared at Samantha in alarm.

"Tell him to be careful who he tells all that to! Someone will try to rob him!" I nudged Ravi.
I knew that just one *lakh* (100,000 rupees) was roughly five hundred pounds. The amount of money he was bragging about having was a lot for Europe, let alone Sri Lanka where the average salary was between 20 – 40,000 rupees per month (between 100-200 pounds). Samantha gave a small smile and waved his hand once Ravi translated my warning.
"No matter. Security camera have."

Although the landlord seemed slightly crazy and pretty eccentric, we agreed to rent out the ground and first floor section of the house, so that we wouldn't have to worry about the two other apartments above. He agreed that we would have absolute privacy, as he was a businessman and had much more pressing issues than worrying about who we invited over for dinner. The only thing he said before handing us the keys was to be aware of one of the neighbours, all of whom were his relations, but one of them could be a bit difficult. He left, insisting that we join him in the new house for dinner soon. On that first night in the new house, I almost cried. It was such a lovely place and I couldn't believe how lucky I was to be there after the multiple hovels I had lived in at University and even after I had graduated. The only downside was the foreboding flight of stairs that we had to clamber up to access the house, which is probably one of the reasons why we were able to rent it for such a reasonable price. "Ready for Sri Pada? Ravindu used to say before we began the ascent.

Known as 'Sri Pada' to Sri Lankans, or 'Adams peak' to Anglophones, was one of two major pilgrimages which most Sri Lankan Buddhists aimed to complete in their lifetime. Although I usually really enjoyed going on hikes, this one was more than a match for my vertically challenged legs. I had also made the trip with Audrey and Beatrice, who played tennis and went to the gym every single day without fail. There wasn't an ounce of fat on either of them. I wasn't exactly obese, but I was far from toned either. However I could have possibly expected to keep up with them I do not know. We rushed up 5,500 steps over a distance of 7 kilometres up to the peak in four hours, arriving at the summit of Sri Lanka's fifth highest mountain just in time for the sunrise, only to be unlucky enough to be met with nothing but gloomy cloud cover, despite all of our hard work.

We were usually able to see incredible sunsets and sunrises just from sitting by a hotel pool in Kandy. The sky in Sri Lanka can be absolutely breath-taking; the oranges, pinks, purples and bright reds streaked across the evening and morning skies like pastels on a canvas. It was like the most wonderful art exhibition; with no entry fee. 'Nuclear fall-out sky' was how I had heard a few people refer to it, and I suppose if the world were ever to end in this way it would indeed be a beautiful end. I supposed that this situation was a bit like the world of work, in the way that it is in fact usually those who work the hardest, like gardeners and cleaners that get very little reward. Those who sit back in their offices and do very little reap the rewards of those who have done all of the physical work.

It was the way down that got me. My legs felt as though they were going to buckle, and if I ever decide to invest in Sri Lanka, it will be to create a zip line from the top of Adam's peak to the bottom. If one were only able to put themselves through this torture once, rather than twice, perhaps one would find it much easier to achieve nirvana.

We also got to know the neighbours in no time. Five houses of Samantha's relations surrounded our house, all bearing families of completely different personalities. Just next to us, there was a family who made elephant statues from papier mâché for a living, and until we were able to learn all of their names, they were known as the 'elephant head people'. They were hard working and friendly, and were two families in the same house, one couple had a ten year old daughter, and the other had a son who was a bit younger. Whenever we walked past their house, the children were always sat at small desks, studying hard.

The house after that contained an older couple, who constantly fought. The man was friendly, and could be seen picking jasmine flowers every morning and evening ready to arrange them as an offering to the Buddha shrine in their house. His wife was also friendly, though before too long we noticed that she had certain likenesses to Mrs Nugawela, very nosy and judgemental. She would occasionally comment that the garden was a little overgrown, or that there was a cobweb on the porch. Out of character, Ravindu had scolded her. Whenever he got annoyed, which was rare, his accent would quickly become a lot more *staccato* and more Indian sounding, which I loved.

"We don't bloody come to your house and make rude comments about tiny things such as that! Why couldn't you ask us how we were, instead of just coming straight away and attacking us with your judgement?" I was grateful at how Ravi had nipped this in the bud, and it didn't happen again after that. We also couldn't remember their names, though we knew that the man had recently had an eye operation, and so Ravindu named him Mr Terminator, and his wife naturally became Mrs Terminator.

The family whom we liked the most lived at the bottom of the stairs by the main road. The older couple had lived and worked in Cyprus as cleaners for 16 years, and they had kindly shown us photographs of their time there and memories. They lived with their son Janidu, who had previously lived in London, and his wife

Akshaya, and they also had two small children. I estimated that the reason we had the most in common with them was that they had been abroad, and therefore had more understanding of those who lived different lifestyles. As we couldn't remember the name of the older couple at first, we fondly named them Mr and Mrs Cyprus, which stuck even when we were more familiar with their real names.

One day, Mrs Cyprus pointed at my arms in shock when I wore a sleeveless dress to school.
"Can a doctor do anything about those? Is it a disease? Does it hurt? Can I catch it?" Her eyes were full of genuine concern, and trying to stop myself from laughing was one of the hardest things I have ever done.
"They're freckles! It happens usually to people who are unlucky enough to have Scottish or Irish genetics. My brother doesn't have them, but I am covered because I take after my mum. Don't worry, you can't catch them, and they don't hurt. It's just that our skin is totally useless against the sun!" My friends and family of course found that story hilarious, and I went to bed that night, grateful for these funny occurrences that I would never encounter had I always stayed in the north east of England.

Ravindu had too made this earlier observation of my freckles, which scattered across my face, arms and legs in their millions.

"You know, you are just like a deer, but the other way round," Ravindu had giggled childishly. "Deers are brown with white spots, and you are white with brown spots!" His voice came to a crescendo, highlighting his excitement at his own theory. As usual, Alina and I had face palmed in exasperation.

Monday 11th June 2018
Kandy, Sri Lanka

I had really settled well into the new house and as good as his word, the landlord had left us well alone. It was now more than six months since the drama had unfolded and Daniel had left. I was now beginning to feel much more positive about the future, and there was nothing at all to be unhappy about. Alina and Ravindu were great company in a lovely spacious house I could have only dreamed of being able to afford anywhere else, we shared the cooking and ate lavish dishes of varying international cuisines each night. We also finally had total privacy and a lovely garden, and the end of the school year was just a couple of weeks away. Unfortunately Vagina had one more nasty trick up his sleeve.

It was lunchtime at school. I had taught three excellent lessons and I was feeling on a real high, when one of the cleaners summoned me to Mr Ranawana's office. Although Mr Ranawana operated an 'open door' policy, I had very rarely been beckoned inside. I merely was curious to learn what the reason for this impromptu conversation would be, yet as soon as I entered his oak panelled sanctuary I noticed with dismay that the expression on his aged face was sombre.

"You called for me, sir?"

"Ah, yes. Please sit down." He paused for a moment, placing his hands together.

"Do you take alcohol?"

What on earth was this about?

"On a Friday night, yes. Though not during the week, no. I like to be fresh for school."

"You haven't taken liquor this morning, or last night?"

"Not at all, no!" I began to feel hurt and outraged. Was he implying that I had some kind of drinking problem? I suppose I may have slightly in the UK due to the insurmountable stress, but certainly not here. I was drinking less than I ever had since trying the stuff in my teens.

"A teacher has come to me this morning and informed me that they can smell alcohol on your breath."

I lost any strand of diplomacy and exploded.

"That's a barefaced lie! I didn't even have a drink last night at all. I can't believe that anybody would say that. May I know who has ever so kindly tried to lose me my job?"

Mr Ranawana shifted uncomfortably in his seat.

"That member of staff does not want to be revealed. It's not professional, no?"

"Those spreading lies of that magnitude are not professional either!" I said hotly. Mr Ranawana gave me

a knowing smile, and leant forward in his chair.
"Be very careful about what you say to whom. I know foreigners go to slightly chilled in the evenings and have a drink. I also take a drink in the evenings. This is a very conservative, very closed society. Many of the staff members have barely been out of Kandy, and they have no idea of what it is like elsewhere. In Sinhala, we have an expression called 'Ling madiyo,' which is a way to describe someone who is like a 'frog in the well'. Be very wary of these people when you speak to them."

I could tell that no matter how much I pushed, Mr Ranawana would not reveal who had stirred up such a vile rumour. In the end he did not need to, as Faiqa did it for me once I returned to the staffroom.
"Lilee, I think you should go to Mr Ranawana again. Vagina is telling people that you're drunk at work."

Sunday 15th July 2018
Negombo, Sri Lanka

After the revelation of Vagina's plot to get me kicked out of Thambili International School, I was looking forward to going back to the comfort of home, mum's cooking, no judgement, and complete social freedom. Bella had enjoyed her visit to Sri Lanka in March so much that she had decided to come back for the whole summer, and work at the Alliance Française, which would greatly help my director friend Alex out. Although I was only able to spend this weekend with her before flying back to Newcastle, it was an absolutely hilarious one.

We had travelled up to Negombo to be close to the airport; so that we could enjoy the weekend together before I flew back home and Bella flew to the Maldives for a few days. As she still had another week before she was due to start teaching at the Alliance, she had decided to spontaneously book a ticket to the Maldives as they were very easily reachable from Sri Lanka, being only a short 45 minute flight away. We had decided to spend the weekend at Jasmine villa, an Ayurveda resort in order to relax before the holidays. It was a gorgeous rustic building; with a beautiful garden and a delicious lunch buffet served in clay pots.

Ayurveda was one of the many wonderful things about this part of the world. Rumoured to have begun in India around 5000 years ago, it is an ancient system of medicine where only natural herbs and remedies are used. The tourism industry has now cottoned on to the business potential of Ayurveda, and so numerous resorts are springing up all over the country. Like many Sri Lankans, Ravindu did not believe in western medicine, and preferred to use traditional remedies, such as *pas panguwa*, which was a concoction of sticks, bark, dried berries and leaves from various trees. Such potions were excellent for treating colds and digestive ailments, and I had been amazed by one of Ravi's mixtures (boiled fenugreek seeds and lime) which had completely resolved the dandruff problem which I had developed in this humid climate.

Another remedy which I was very impressed with had been the turmeric and beeswax hair removal cream, yielding better results than Veet or Nair, but without the putrid stench and sting that these chemical rich creams seem to generate. Ravi also made the best hangover cure in the form of lime juice with crushed ginger, sugar, salt and pepper. He really could have been a traditional doctor in a past life. Despite my great interest and approval of such things, I did feel that Ravi had gone a bit too far when he insisted on checking himself into an Ayurvedic hospital following a leg injury while playing football.

"What are they going to do if it's broken, put some leaves on it?" I had asked him, and was met with little response but a glowering expression on his handsome face.

At Jasmine Villa, Bella and I opted for full body massages and the *Shirodara* treatment, a blissfully relaxing experience which involves warm oil dribbling onto your forehead over a fifteen or twenty minute period. The oil is released from small pewter cauldrons which hang above your head and makes for a truly unique escapade where one can be completely alone with their thoughts. We had a lovely day and once darkness fell, in true Bella and Lilee fashion we decided to head out for some farewell drinks.

Once we returned to Jasmine villa at around midnight and ever so slightly crapulous, there was not a soul in sight. The only other identifiable living and breathing organisms in sight were two vibrant green birds, who were sitting quietly in their cage, which is not how Bella saw them.

"They're prisoners, getting the same treatment as mad axe murderers or rapists. Let's release them at once, so they can be free!"

I nervously looked around for a security guard or cameras, but my quick scan yielded no results.

"I agree they should be in the wild. But what if we get caught? They'll throw us out onto the street."

"If they're Buddhists they shouldn't be doing this anyway, being cruel to animals. In fact no-one should be!"

With a jerk and a wrench, Bella tore off the cage door. It should have been a beautiful moment, where the bird extended its wings gracefully, and soared away to its deserving freedom; however it just remained sitting in its cage, staring at us both with utmost confusion.

"Come on, you silly bugger!" Bella reached inside to try to show the bamboozled bird the way, but it wouldn't budge.

"It's been deprived of its freedom for so long, it doesn't even know that there's a whole world out there beyond this awful barbaric cage!" Bella cried, and eventually after much persuasion and a shower of bird shit later, the bird flew away.

"How ungrateful was he? It never happens like that on films, does it?"

After the anti-climax of our 'rescue', we decided to call it a night and head to bed, as Bella had her flight to catch in the early hours.

After she departed in a Tuk Tuk bound for the airport and I waved her off, I went back to sleep and was met with a text message from her when I woke up, which read:

"I only flipping managed to fly all the way to the Maldives with bird shit down my dress didn't I? Only realised halfway through the flight."

Although I was alone, I doubled up in fits of laughter for a few minutes, before realising the gravity of what had happened the night before. I hurriedly double checked that the door to the hotel room was locked, fearing that on discovery of the broken bird cage, several burly security guards would be charging through the door to arrest and deport me. I messaged Alina and Subashi with details of my predicament, hoping that they would put my mind at ease, though they actually managed to do the exact opposite.

"From what you've described, it sounds like an *Eclectus*. They can be worth 200,000 rupees – almost a thousand pounds!"

"There's no way a bird could possibly cost that much. Who on earth in their right mind would pay that much for a bird anyway when you could just get something like a common budgie? They're just as pretty." I was sure that Alina was over exaggerating; she had to be having me on. To my dismay, a quick Google search confirmed that she was correct. The photograph of the *Eclectus* parrot matched exactly my memory of the luminous green bird Bella had freed the previous evening. Unless I was very much mistaken, and had been wearing bird beer goggles, there was no way in a million years that the owner of this exotic pet was going to let me off scot free. Bella was now all the way in the Maldives, and it was surely going to be I who would cop for it.

I prepared to phone Ravindu to explain my fate, and say goodbye to him and Sri Lanka forever. What a terrible ending this would be. I was sure that there are much more interesting tales than this out there, for example *'British teacher gets deported for coming to work naked'* or *'Briton burns down school abroad, international man hunt under way'*. Not something like *'British teacher imprisoned for rare bird release and brutal sabotage of aviary.'*

As I had expected, Ravi had been his usual cool and collected self on the phone, and had convinced me not to worry. He was already on the bus on the way up to Negombo to meet me as planned for my last day and night in Sri Lanka before flying back to the UK for a few weeks. When he arrived a couple of hours later, he had his adorable cheeky grin plastered on his sweet face. "You know the cage has been taken down, and is sitting in the security guard's hut? The funniest thing is that still no-one is there!"

My hand flew to my mouth and I winced with dread. They already knew the bird was missing; I had to find a way to do a runner.

"Shall we go and just explain to them what happened? Or shall we make a run for it while the security guard is still nowhere to be seen?"

"Maybe he's gone to call in the armed forces or extra back up," said Ravi with a naughty glint in his eye.

"Will you take this seriously? Its fine for you, you're Sri Lankan, they can't deport you! What if they cancel my visa over this?"

"It's Sri Lanka, Lilee. Trust me, they really won't care. I'm sure that bird will have just been a common parrot. If it was so special they wouldn't have left it unprotected for so long! I think the best course of action is that we do nothing."

As always, Ravi turned out to be right. Nobody batted an eyelid even when we paid the bill for the room and the treatments we had enjoyed that day. As I said goodbye to him at the airport, the realisation of how much I would miss him hit me like the force of tidal wave. We embraced tightly, and I inhaled his scent deeply for the last time for the foreseeable future. I couldn't bear to let him go. Even as soon as he released me every cell of me ached for the warmth of his body. "Look after Bella when she gets back, and I'll see you in a few weeks!" As I walked through the departures with tears racing down my cheeks, the airport staff looked at me with bemusement. It must be so interesting to work in an airport, witnessing hundreds of ecstatic hello's and heartfelt goodbyes, one day after another.

Chapter 14 - Surangani

Monday 22nd October 2018
Kandy, Sri Lanka

I had returned from my holidays to mayhem. The number of students taking German for IGCSE and A level had significantly increased over the past two years, and as a result our timetables reciprocated this trend. For the first time in the twenty year history of Thambili International School, it appeared that we needed another German teacher in addition to Belinda and me. This should have of course been organised over the summer, however the management in typical tightwad style had decided to 'see how we would manage'. This had resulted in both of us having timetables similar to what I had had back in the UK. The situation was so tight that we were even forced to merge some classes, for instance, Year 12 with Year 11, resulting in us desperately trying to teach IGCSE and A level syllabuses at the same time, whilst also attempting to practise speaking during the lesson.

Belinda asked me to search far and wide within the digital realm to see if we could find anyone well trained and qualified who would be interested in coming at such short notice. To my amazement, within a couple of days of posting a query on a Facebook group for teachers, my inbox was positively overflowing with talented professionals who could also offer French as well as German, and Belinda was thrilled.

Unfortunately, the management were not as enthusiastic. They insisted that as there were already two foreign teachers in the languages department, (Belinda and I) we would have to find a local Sri Lankan teacher to fill the role so that it would not become too unbalanced in comparison to other departments. What they really meant to say is that they didn't want to pay the extra salary that is required when employing a teacher with actual teacher training.

It is no secret of course that foreign teachers are paid salaries which are exponentially higher than local teachers in the host country, which is grossly unfair. I am not talking 10% more, but more likely 10 times more. The poor standard of pay is understandably very demotivating for the local teachers, and as a result the teaching profession has become extremely stagnated in many countries, of which Sri Lanka is sadly no exception. There is little opportunity nor demand to provide adequate teacher training, and in many government schools, a sign of a good teacher is simply how well they wear their sari.

Each class can consist of fifty or sixty students, meaning that working from the textbook in silence or copying from the board are pretty much the only things that can be done, and the idea of students even asking questions or challenging the information that they are given is most unwelcome. The students still live in fear of the cane, which was banned in European schools around fifty years ago. This has sadly resulted in generations who are unable to challenge authority or think for themselves critically or logically. In the end, this is what the politicians and religious leaders want, so they can continue to get away with their reckless squandering of taxpayer's money with nobody daring to challenge them.

The difference between a Sri Lankan who went to a government school and an international school is insane; it is almost as though they are worlds apart and remain so throughout adulthood. People I have met from a government school background are often not at all confident to speak to me, and are very quick to judge any way of life or appearance which is different to theirs. Those who were lucky enough to go to international schools are almost always very confident, opinionated, chatty and open minded to other ways of life. It is no secret that the Sri Lankan government does not particularly like international schools, and so they removed the right for students who have studied in an international school to go to a Sri Lankan university, which has contributed to a massive brain drain of the brighter and more confident students going to universities abroad.

Following the request of the management, we advertised in the local newspaper for a German teacher. Had we been in Colombo, we would have had no problem, however we knew that finding a German teacher in the Kandy area, let alone a good one, was going to be like finding a blue coconut in a rainforest. Belinda interviewed Surangani, who was the one applicant we had, who said that she had a degree in German from a University in the north of the island. Despite a few spelling mistakes, her interview lesson had also shown promise, and she had shown a real enthusiasm for being in the classroom. We hoped that our problem was now solved.

How credible this degree was, I do not know, however we rapidly discovered to our dismay that she could speak only a few words of German and English. This led to our usually impeccably behaved students tearing her apart within the first few weeks, and multiple complaints from parents, who were understandably furious that they were now paying the most expensive school fees in the area for substandard teaching. I found it quite difficult to hold it together when I was met with an irate parent and I quote:
"Having her teaching German is like going to Pizza Hut and asking for KFC."

For the first few weeks, it was beginning to look like Surangani was starting to sink, and so I decided to help her as much as I could and mentor her. This situation was not her fault; she was merely a product of the government school system. I also remembered how my start to teaching had been far from easy once I had completed my training in a supportive school, and I recalled how life saving and necessary that support could be. I asked her to observe two of my lessons per week, and I would watch one of her lessons per week and give her constructive advice. It dawned on me then how lucky I was to have been able to observe so many talented teachers during my training year, and been able to learn so much and have professional advice given so willingly. Teachers here are completely on their own once they get a teaching post.

Surangani was only in her early twenties; young and enthusiastic and very smiley. Despite being from a tiny village, she was very open to new ideas and loved to create attractive visual aids and games for the students, which was great and I told her so. The problem was her spelling, and the errors were so persistent I wondered if she was dyslexic. I was reluctant to ask as I did not want to cause any offence; as such things are not recognised nor discussed in many Asian countries.

Ultimately, no parent wishes to accept that there is anything 'wrong' with their child and risk 'losing face' in society. There were a number of students enrolled in our school who had benefited from teaching assistants when they had lived in the UK or Australia for example, and sadly there was no such provision for them here at all. The fact that Thambili International School had the reputation of being the best school with the smallest class sizes in the area was sufficient to satisfy their parents that they were getting the best possible education, which is in fact probably true as the alternative options would be even worse.

Although there were a few teaching assistants when I taught back at Panaculty Academy, unfortunately as is the case in many academies, they are run like businesses by management who often have zero pedagogical background, and do not understand that throwing money at improving the facilities and marketing the aesthetically pleasing aspects of the school are not the best things to be done. The greatest investment that should be made is on human resources: teachers and teaching assistants. At Panaculty Academy, there were probably more technological facilities than on the international space station, but in order to pay for all of this, the management had decided to roll out staff redundancies in order to cut costs. This meant that I lost my wonderful teaching assistant. With her help, I had been able to just about manage to battle through the lessons and keep children with very severe behavioural issues entertained. Once she was gone, the classroom atmosphere would be quite comparable to Chernobyl, as I certainly was like a nuclear reactor going into meltdown trying to manage a situation which was frankly unmanageable, no matter how fancy the school looked, and how many state of the art gadgets there were.

On reflection, I found it interesting as well as sad that teaching assistants were undervalued in both schools, albeit for differing reasons. At Thambili International School, teaching assistants have never even been considered, as special needs for most Sri Lankans are swept under the carpet and out of sight. At Panaculty Academy they just didn't want to pay for them.

The issue of Surangani's spelling really came to light during the report writing period at the end of the first term. At Thambili International, all of the reports are still written by hand and there is one page per child with sections for all of the different subjects. This means that whenever a mistake is made by anybody, the whole report has to be rewritten again. By now I was well aware that the time of report writing is a particularly tense and stressful process, and so I suggested to Surangani that she could write out drafts and I would correct any spelling issues before she entered the reports for real and quickly made many enemies amongst the staff. To my dismay, she politely rejected my suggestion.

"Why on earth would I write them twice, when I can just write them once?" She laughed and smiled, wobbling her head as though I was clearly out of my tree. I had too many things to do to protest; she would surely learn the hard way. Sure enough, a few days later there were teachers queuing up at her desk, passively aggressively handing her the reports to write out again, that they had completed for the second or maybe third

time. The usual errors of 'she is making a good progress' or 'he is making a bad attitude' were now accentuated with 'he is a pleasent fellow' or 'she is definately improveing.' I bit back the urge to say,
"In the end, you had to write them twice anyway, Surangani!"

Report writing at Panaculty Academy had also been a real challenge, but in a different way. I had taken great pride in writing the reports, as I remembered how much attention my parents would pay to mine when I was younger. I worked late into the night before the report deadline and submitted them on time, confident that there was not one snag in the fabric. Louise Haughty had ambled into my classroom early the next morning holding print outs of the reports, and my heart sank as I realised that I should have known better than to think that there wouldn't be something that she would find to criticise.
"The problem here is the language that you have used...the parents in this community will not understand it. You need to tone it down to their level."
"But we're a school! Surely it's our job and responsibility to set a high standard, particularly when using language? I'm sure they've all heard of a dictionary."
"We can't send them out like that. There'll be complaints. You'll have to do them again, by the end of today."
It took every cell of me not to swear at this recalcitrant

woman, and I begrudgingly began to alter my beautifully written reports to dumb down and patronise the local community, which were basically what my orders had been. Phrases like 'he is making exceptional progress' became 'he is doing very well' and 'she must apply herself fully' became 'she must work harder.' 'He must address his lackadaisical attitude' became 'he must pay more attention in class' and 'she works with diligence' became 'she works well.' Although we at least had the luxury of completing the reports on the computer as opposed to writing them by hand, it was still rather an unpleasant process.

I returned that day to an empty house. Having rewritten a colossal sum of reports I was absolutely exhausted and had rather hoped that Ravindu would have taken the initiative to make something to eat. He hadn't contacted me all day, which was very unusual as his daily attentiveness had taken a lot of getting used to as opposed to Daniel's grunts and grumbles. I tried calling him, but to no avail. I settled for some cheese on toast and decided to read a book, though the words just rolled past my eyes like the credits at the end of a film. Something just wasn't right – the only reason he would have for his lack of radio contact would be that his phone battery was dead, and it was ringing perfectly fine. As the hot and humid weather was not at all helping my rapidly declining mood, I decided to go for a refreshing swim at a nearby hotel where Ravindu and I had a membership.

As I walked into the lobby of the Grand Kandyan Hotel something made me stop dead in my tracks. In the main ballroom on the ground floor a wedding was taking place, and the sign clearly read:
"Celebrating the marriage of Ravindu and Surangani. Monday 22nd October 2018." My jaw nearly hit the floor. What a co-incidence. I slyly snapped a photo and sent it to Ravindu, but there was still no sign of any activity. It was very rare for him to disappear from the domain of cyberspace like this, and I hastily plunged into the cold pool in an attempt to distract myself from worrying of his whereabouts. An hour later as I got ready to leave for home, I checked my phone again. Still nothing. Trying not to overreact I returned home, passing the wedding which was now in full flow. Ladies milled around the entrance to the ballroom, clad in beautiful and vibrantly coloured saris taking as many selfies as their camera phone memories would permit. The men hung around outside, discreetly sharing cigarettes and conversation which would certainly not be deemed appropriate for such esteemed ladies. I tried to catch a glimpse of the bride and groom, a tiny cluster of particles within me terrified that they would in fact be my Ravindu and Surangani from school, but they were nowhere to be seen.

Once clambering up the stairs to the house, I decided that the best course of action was to return to the book I was reading in the hope that it would take my mind away from Ravindu and where on earth he could be. I curled up on the bed, hoping that I would find solace in printed words from an author other than Ravi.

He eventually replied at around nine in the evening. 'I'm on my way back now babu,' the message read. 'I'll explain everything when I get there and hope you will understand'.
Hope I will understand? Now I was really confused. I would have had something ready for him to eat, but frankly with his mysterious whereabouts he had not earned this luxury today. I wondered what on earth there was to understand; had he decided to move away somewhere else, or found a job somewhere else maybe? I never could have predicted the real reason.

When Ravi returned, he was his usual smiling self which settled me a little. That was, until he came out with it. "I've agreed to marry one of the girls that my aunt found and I met her this evening. Just know that it won't change anything between us at all, it's just a practicality to secure my future."

I couldn't believe what I was hearing. My worst imaginable nightmare was coming true; or maybe it was karma for how things had ended with Daniel.

"But you said...you said that it wouldn't happen, and that she couldn't make you do anything!" I began to cry as the world spun and blurred through the fresh painful tears in my eyes. Ravi tried to grab my hands, but I swatted him away.

"It won't change *anything* between us, I promise!" he insisted.

"It'll change everything! Why are you doing this? How can you marry someone you don't love, or barely know? Its madness!"

"Madness that your people brought here in the colonial times, may I remind you. Before the British came we had a completely different system from all of this matrimonial stuff. I have to think about securing my future Lilee...if you leave Sri Lanka one day, and I'm left with nothing... it will be too late to do anything. I don't have my parents to fix me up, and I have to take this stress away from my aunt, who worries what will become of me one day." Ravi paused for breath, and I could see in his face that he now understood that I did not see this situation as simply as he did.

"Her family will pay a really good dowry you see, and I'll be able to fix up the house with no more money worries for the rest of my life. Her parents are both head teachers of a village school and she's a teacher – you may even get along in the end – ow!"

Unable to hold back at that last comment, I slapped Ravindu's smooth cheek hard.

"How dare you even suggest that I meet her! What planet are you on?!" I yelled at him, my vocal chords strangled with the fear and realisation of what was happening.

"The thing is Lilee, you already have met her. She knows

275

and understands the situation between us, and has agreed that as long as we are very discreet, nothing about our relationship has to change. Remember this marriage is not for love, but financial stability and practicality, which I'll remind you again is how many marriages are here. Remember your friend who was gay and in a relationship, but also married a girl he didn't love and had a child? We have to keep our families happy and money in our pockets at the end of the day."
Ravi had a hold of both my hands now, gazing at me with sadness in his eyes as it sunk in that I would not accept this at all.
"I can't ever be without you Lilee. You know that."

"How have I already met her? Who is she? Subashi?"
The shock of Ravindu getting married was enough – but the fact that it was to someone I knew was a real double whammy.
"She works at your school I believe. Your new German teacher."
"Surangani!? You can't be serious! Tell me this is a joke!"
"She's very nice, Lilee. Remember she knows about us and is kind and understanding. Just look at it like a business transaction; I get the dowry from her parents, and she inherits the house and land, and we both get the status. Come to think of it, you won't have to worry about anyone else making a move on me anymore, if they all know I'm married!"

I folded my arms. No matter how much I loved him, and would have done anything for him, this I could not tolerate.

"Then we move far away from here and I'll get a job somewhere else. I can't stay here and be nice to her at work every day, knowing that she is married to you. It'll be absolutely unbearable. I can't believe you're prepared to even put me through all this. You're only thinking of yourself here!"

Ravindu looked at me glumly.

"You won't really leave will you? The preparations are already underway, so I can't back out now. We had our horoscopes read today, and so the *poruwa* is scheduled for two weeks' time, the day and time that the astrologer advised."

The *poruwa* is the ceremony where various marriage rituals are performed, such as tying the little fingers of the bride and groom together, feeding each other milk rice, and the groom draping the bride with material, which symbolises how he will provide for her. A ceremony which Surangani would enjoy and I wouldn't. I wouldn't even be in the country by then.

"If you loved me, you wouldn't even consider this, just like you said a few months ago. You can't possibly expect me to stay. Right now, you need to leave. I need to be alone and get used to being alone."

Ravindu tried to convince me otherwise at first, but eventually he gave in, realising that the damage was done and there was nothing that he could possibly say that would change my mind. When I was certain that he had left, I cried and cried, more than I ever had before. Later that night I drifted off to sleep, after searching for beautiful cats who I could adopt in an attempt to curb my eternal cycle of heartbreak and loneliness.

I woke with a start in the early hours, drenched in sweat and tears. The wedding! I fumbled around blindly in the dark, my hands shaking to find clothes as quickly as possible. I didn't know how I was going to do it, but I had to get there as quickly as possible and stop it...
A dark shape stirred in the bed next to me.
"Babu? What's the matter?"
I suddenly stopped dead.
"Ravi? But...the wedding..." The fragmented world shifted gradually back into focus.
"What wedding? Did you have a crazy dream?"
My breathing slowed, and I came back to reality again.
"It was a dream... are you sure?"
Ravi laughed, pulling me into his arms and kissing me on the head.
"So silly you are! I think it must be the wedding sign that you saw at the Grand Kandyan that sent you on a really weird trip."
"Why didn't you let me know where you were today? I was worried." As I descended back to planet Earth from my eerie and uncomfortably realistic dream, my initial relief that Ravindu in fact wasn't getting married vanished as I swiftly remembered that I should still be a

little cross with him for not keeping in touch.

"So where were you? It's not like you to be so unreachable and elusive! For all I know, you probably were in the middle of arranging a marriage!" Ravindu laughed even harder, his mouth splitting open like a can of beans.

"I was at Ruwan's place for band practice today, remember? I left my phone on charge and then we went to visit his uncle and I totally forgot about it. I should have messaged you from Ruwan's phone though, I'm really sorry Lilee. I didn't think you would worry this much!"

"Me neither." I said, beginning to relax a little. It was true how I had never really fretted so much over someone before. I wrapped my arms tightly around Ravi, so grateful for his warm body; for his heart that continued to beat, for his brilliant mind, for his good nature and his unbeatable humour. It was that day I knew for certain I could not live without him, and the thought of losing him was insufferable.

Sunday 7th April 2019
Bandaranaike International Airport,
Colombo, Sri Lanka

Poking his head through the hole of the cardboard cut-out of a Sri Lankan national team cricket player, Ravindu grinned boyishly outside the duty free store. The excitement in the air was electric, and even the security official had smiled warmly when he had taken Ravindu's passport, and seen the Vietnamese visa inside. We had worried that he would not get the visa in time, as we had handed his passport along with the application form to the Vietnamese embassy in early February, yet because of Donald Trump and Kim Jong Un's famous and very highly publicised meeting, they had put a block on issuing tourist visas from certain countries until the talks were over, which unfortunately had included Sri Lanka.

"It's probably because of the war that our passports are so useless," Ravindu had mused.

"The old president, Mahinda Rajapaksa, ordered all of the international organisations to get out during and after the war, so this must be their payback."

It was indeed an issue. The Sri Lankan passport was ranked 178th out of 199 nations in 2019, which meant going anywhere was extremely difficult for Ravindu. Getting a visa for most people who are lucky enough to be born in a western country is simply a formality, and a very easily completed process. Ravindu had stapled his new passport to two of his old previous passports which contained expired visas from a variety of Asian countries as well as Australia. I persisted that surely this was not necessary, however Ravi argued that visas were extremely valuable and to be shown at every possible opportunity.

We sat in the airport bar with our lonely planet guide, excitedly planning out our two week adventure.

I was particularly excited to go to Da Lat, a hill station where the climate was said to be similar to that of Nuwara Eliya in Sri Lanka which was one of our favourite places, mainly because it was one of the few places my ginger gene skin could handle. I had actually burnt in Nuwara Eliya once, which was a fact that was found hilarious by all. The thing that we were both looking forward to the most was both being foreigners together in a country and no longer being seen as a 'beach boy' and 'sex tourist' couple.

Ravindu would always say, 'people who mind don't matter. And the people who matter don't mind.' He was usually much more optimistic about things than I was, and would cheerily remark that it was often the fact that we were going against everyone that would keep us strong. We were also blessed with a few good friends who we believed were genuinely happy for us.

However, it was never easy automatically being viewed by those who did not know us as the 'illegitimate fun seekers.' When we had travelled to the south coast together once for a week, it had been extremely difficult to find accommodation as many people did not want a mixed couple or a perceived 'beach boy and tourist ensemble' staying in their guesthouse. Of course, in the larger and more faceless hotels there was no problem but that was a luxury which you had to pay ten times the price of a guesthouse for. Another time when we had gone to Arugam Bay for a long weekend with a group of teachers from the same school, all nine of us European teachers had walked into the beach party at no cost, whereas poor Ravindu had been stopped and asked to pay 5000 rupees (approximately 25 pounds). Ravindu had previously been unaware of such unfair treatment, and whenever he saw a man and woman who were not of the same complexion he would yell in delight:

'meeeeeeexed cappel!' (mixed couple!)

We both had waited with a degree of impatience to experience some time out of Sri Lanka, and particularly Kandy together, and although it was our home we did sometimes question the longevity of our happiness there.

However, I continue to adore my school, my colleagues (well, most of them) and my students, and the thought of leaving Thambili International is at times too much to bear. Ravindu is still perfectly happy jamming along with his band at the weekends. If one had told me how tremendously my life was going to change back on that miserable night in October 2015, I would never in a million years have believed them. I would never for one moment have imagined that I would fall in love with a Buddhist rock star, that I would have learned how to wear and teach in a sari, and certainly never that I would swap wine for curry for breakfast.

Epilogue

Sunday 21st April 2019
Hanoi, Vietnam

At the time of writing this diary, and being at the point where I had decided to bring the story to a happy close, the unthinkable happened, whilst 'Ravindu' and I were in our hotel room in Hanoi. Although I wanted my diary to be read in the same humorous, light hearted and happy way that I now view my life, I want to mention this horrible ordeal which will hopefully go down in the history books that Sri Lanka fought back against this atrocity with peace, not hatred.

At around eleven a.m., we still lay on the soft mattress in the comfortable air conditioned room, which protected us against the suffocating pollution of Hanoi, unable to stop laughing at the events which had happened the night before. We had met up with a couple from Newcastle who we had met on the Ha Long bay cruise, and watched Newcastle beat Southampton 3 – 1 in the football match. Naturally, spirits had been high and a great night had been had by all. We had also met another Sri Lankan who was from Negombo, but had moved to Canada when he was 11 he said, because of the war and the LTTE (Liberation Tigers of Tamil Eelam).

This morning, we were laughing at the idiocy of a Londoner who had overheard our conversations, and had butted in with "so are you guys Sinhalese? What you did to the Tamils was unbelievable. I watched the Channel 4 documentary and studied it for my degree." In typical Ravindu fashion, he had replied with: "Hey! You look like Jay Z!" The Londoner had drawn in his

283

breath faster than those around him who were breathing in laughing gas from balloons, pulled a face, and walked off in fury. "I still can't believe you called him Jay Z. He's like the ugliest person ever!" I buried my face in the pillow, howling.

"I thought it was a compliment!" grinned Ravindu.

One had to admire how he could turn any negative situation into laughter. It was his happy and undefeatable personality that made him so loved by many, even in spite of the adversities he had already faced in his youth, he just wanted to crack a (terrible) joke. If I had responded to the Londoner first, he would have had a rant that the Channel 4 documentary was in fact extremely one sided, not one Sinhalese person having been interviewed. And can you hold an entire population of people responsible for the actions of the government?

Anyway, back to this morning. My phone pinged all of a sudden, and it was a message from my friend Kim back in the UK. "I've just heard about the attacks in Sri Lanka," she wrote. "It's awful. I hope you both are ok! xxx" From that moment, everything changed for the foreseeable future. We looked at each other in horror and shock, hoping that whatever the damage was, it was very minimal. Once we switched on the TV, it was indeed breaking world news. The death toll started at around 50, and then it rose, and rose, and rose. Bomb after bomb after bomb was reported. Three in churches, packed with worshippers celebrating Easter

Sunday; and three in the Kingsbury, Shangri-La, and Cinnamon Grand hotels, some of the most prestigious hotels in Colombo. My hand flew to my mouth, as I realised that some of our friends who ran the Millennium Elephant Foundation had said they were at an Easter brunch event at the Cinnamon Grand Hotel this morning. They had invited us, but we weren't due to fly back from Vietnam until tomorrow (Monday). I hastened to call Jade, who had invited us to the brunch, and I feared the worst.

I felt as though I had been transported back in time to 26th June 2015, when a lone gunman had murdered 38 tourists on the beach in Port-el-Kantaoui, Tunisia, on the same streets I had walked just a year earlier. One of the first victims to be named was Carly Lovett, who had been my classmate at school. Although we hadn't been close, and had lost touch since leaving school, with the exception of bumping into her on one random night out in Lincoln when I went down there to visit a few old friends, the fact remained that someone I shared memories with, some of my teenage years with, someone who I had shared sneaky cigarettes together with in Richmond park before school some mornings, someone who had stuck up for me against bullies when she really didn't have to, had been brutally murdered. And for what reason? My heart went out, and still goes out, to her family, friends, and her fiancé, who I also remember from those Richmond park mornings. They were childhood sweethearts and had recently bought a house together, so I heard. When I thought of the pain he in particular must be feeling, my heart split, and my throat burned in agony for him.

I had been a total mess for weeks, trying to book flights to Syria to go and finish ISIS off myself, writing angry, tear stained letters to Abu-Bakr-Al-Baghdadi, the leader of ISIS, even Google translating into Arabic the words: why? Just why? I could not make any sense of the situation, could not draw up any conclusion, or reason for this to happen. School back in Stanley was completely unsupportive, maybe even worse so than when I lost Zizou-Wazizi. The history teacher, keen to brown nose her way up to senior management level had noticed my erratic behaviour and instead of talking to me about it, had reported me to the head teacher, who had coldly said: "remember what you do for a living." I mentioned this when I handed in my resignation letter in November, stating: "As teachers, we cannot openly grieve for ones we have lost in such an awful way? I cannot be a machine with no feelings, and I wish you luck in finding one."

So here I was, feeling the same shock and fear all over again. I kept calling Jade, but there was no answer. I bombarded her with messages on WhatsApp and Facebook, but still no answer. I refused to believe it, I could not believe it, that this was happening. Not in Sri Lanka. Not where I had felt so safe and welcome for the last three years. It had just been voted the number one travel destination in the world for 2019 by lonely planet. What would happen now? Would people still come? What of the thousands, if not millions, who depended on tourism for their daily bread?

"I've got a horrible feeling...I really have..." I shook my head, my whole body shaking, before bursting into tears.

"Hey, hey hey! Don't cry now! She will be still asleep or in a pool somewhere else. That'll be what it is, she will have had a good drink last night, Saturday night, and she'll be asleep still!" Ravindu wrapped his arms around me, trying to protect us both verbally and physically for what terrible news may be about to come. The television blared on in the background, now showing photographs and video footage of the damage from the bomb blasts. We both knew having the news on was making us both feel even worse, but we could not turn it off for fear of new news. I gradually grew more and more hysterical with worry, imagining my friend with whom I had had a stupid argument with only a few weeks ago, lying somewhere bloodied on a pavement, lifeless. I tried to push such vile images out of my mind, yet I could not.

After what seemed an eternity, Jade phoned. Although I am not, and never will be religious, I thanked God silently as I spoke to her. They had been on their way to the Cinnamon Grand Hotel, running late, and heard the news on the radio, and had turned back. They were all in shock, and said they were going to have a day of drinking to numb their minds and try to forget how close they had come to death. It is these moments, when such horrific events occur, when one realises just how fragile life is, and how important it is to value each person who means something to you in your life, and tell them that while you can.

For the rest of the afternoon, we watched the news non-stop, in silence, numb and exhausted from disbelief and shock. Two more bombs exploded in the suburbs of Colombo. Social media was blocked in Sri Lanka to stop the spread of hate, so everyone went quiet for a while before they could download a VPN app and get back on Facebook and WhatsApp. We had planned to spend our last day in Hanoi shopping, and to watch the water puppet show, one of the many things for which Vietnam is famous. Instead we stayed put in the hotel room, unable to move. Later in the day it was announced that the NTJ 'National Thowheed Jamath', a previously unknown group, was responsible for the attack. ISIS had claimed responsibility, yet as the CNN reporter said, they often make a claim for things they had nothing to do with. There was the potential that ISIS had inspired the NTJ to carry out the attacks, yet it was still them who had done it. 'Wealthy Sri Lankan Muslims, the sons of a millionaire spice trader', said the news. I thought back to March the previous year, in 2018, when violence had erupted amongst the Buddhists and Muslims close to our home, causing schools to close and a curfew to be imposed for a week. That was absolutely nothing compared to this. What on earth were we about to come back to?

My thoughts turned to school. I worried for Faiqa, the head of English and her family, and her daughters Suli and Aisha, who were so intelligent and wonderful. Would they be safe? Would they face retaliatory comments and even violence? I worried for my students and their families too, not now just that they were safe from the attacks, but that they would be safe from any future attacks. I thought about Nusha, Fathima and Zafra, my amazing Year 8 girls, who just a month ago had wowed me with a professional presentation about health and fitness in German. They were Muslim. I thought about Ahmed, Abdel, and Salman, my Year 10 boys who were insanely clever, and had a cracking sense of humour. Ahmed had also been affected by the violence in Kandy in March 2018, and they had even had to leave their home for the safety of a hotel for a few days. They were Muslim. Would it be the innocent, who would pay for the crimes of the wicked?

"If they attack a Buddhist temple, we will be facing another war," murmured Ravindu. "People will go absolutely mental if that happens."

We spent our last evening in Vietnam both speculating at what might happen now, while not wanting to speculate. We barely slept, our eyes closed, but brains in full whirr.

Monday, 22nd April 2019
Hanoi, Vietnam

The following morning we checked out of the hotel like zombies, and made the journey to the airport, watching the Vietnamese go about their daily lives, making street food like Banh mi and Bun Chao, swooping through the traffic on their agile scooters, oblivious to the horror that was fresh and raw almost two thousand miles to the west of them. We were even more reluctant to leave than we had been before we had learned of what had happened. As we checked in for our flight to Bangkok, where we would have to wait a few hours before our onwards flight back to Colombo, I received a message from a friend who told me that a pipe bomb had been found in the Bandaranaike airport in Colombo. I clicked on the attached news link.
'A 6 foot pipe bomb, packed with C-4 explosives, was located and detonated by the Sri Lankan armed forces close to the airport today,' it read.

Bomb, explosives, detonated, armed forces... these were all words used when describing a war zone. Not the place where I had lived so happily and peacefully for years. My brain felt like a jelly, or maybe a *watalappan,* with a bee stuck inside, humming.

We had a long, long, wait in Bangkok. The airport WIFI didn't work, so we had no way of finding out any updates. Everything was ridiculously overpriced. When I went to ask the sullen woman behind the glass counter at the currency exchange how many Thai Bhat twenty pounds would fetch, she was extremely unhelpful. For some unknown and probably obscure reason the bar near the departure gate would not serve a glass of wine. It was hard to believe that just two weeks earlier, we had left the airport brimming with excitement, our radiating smiles unfaltering. Two weeks later, and we weren't just upset to come home after a great holiday, but dreading what lay ahead of us. We boarded the plane after a short delay. Apparently they were changing the plane's tyre. Two Air Marshalls, in jackets emblazoned with 'special security' on their backs searched us as we stepped onto the walkway. I had heard of an Air Marshall before, but had never seen one. They stood guard robustly during the flight, one at either end of the almost empty plane, which shuddered and rattled in anguish as it heaved itself off the ground at breakneck speed, as though the plane itself was reluctant to fly to a destination which had all of a sudden been deemed dangerous. Despite the best efforts of the turbulent air the two Air Marshalls didn't move an inch. They made the situation even more frightening. We clasped our hands together, unsure of what to expect once we returned to the country we had left so happily just two weeks ago.

Acknowledgements

My dear mum, who has a heart of gold and I am sorry that it took so long for me to value it.

My aunty Vicky and uncle Simon, who taught me words like 'spurious' and helped me to develop my vocabulary over the years which became enough to write a book.

My brother Ben. Despite the fact we are like chalk and cheese, I know we are always there for each other.

Kate and Richie, who listened and supported me through all of my dramas over and over again, and were always good friends through the worst of it all.

Bex, who has to be the funniest, strongest, and most kind hearted person I have ever met.

All of my 'motley crew' uni gang! Thank you all for the unforgettable and never-ending laughs. I can't go into specifics, or I'll have to write another book!

Suzi Bewell & Liz Black, who took a chance with me, and did not just train me as a teacher, but inspired me so much with their unstoppable positivity and love of teaching languages.

Christina Mueller-Stewart, who taught me German as well as how to 'Stammtisch.'

Shashi & Anja: my Kandyan partners in crime and fellow food enthusiasts. Thank you for putting up with my incessant whining and always telling it how it is!

*Belinda, Faiqa, and all other staff at Thambili International School. Thank you all for your continuous support and encouragement, which is something that should never be taken for granted.

*Staff in the Humanities department at Haggerty Academy. Thank you for taking me under your wings and looking after me so well, even though I had already made the decision to move away.

*Mr Ranawana, to whom I will always be eternally grateful for his stories and wisdom.

My grandma and granddad who are sadly no longer with us. Thank you for everything you ever did.

My dear Amila who showed me what real love was, and continues to show me what love is every single day.

*Anonymised names. You all know who you are.

For your reference

Teacher's standards (UK government guidelines)
PART ONE - TEACHING

1. Set high expectations which challenge, motivate, and inspire pupils

2. Promote good progress and outcomes by pupils

3. Demonstrate good subject and curriculum knowledge

4. Plan and teach well-structured lessons

5. Adapt teaching to respond to the strengths and needs of all pupils

6. Make accurate and productive use of assessment

7. Manage behaviour effectively to ensure a good and safe learning environment

8. Fulfil wider professional responsibilities

PART TWO – PERSONAL AND PROFESSIONAL CONDUCT

- Treat pupils with dignity and build relationships rooted on mutual respect

- Safeguard pupil's well-being

- Show tolerance and respect for the rights of others

- Do not undermine fundamental British values, for instance the rule of law, democracy, individual liberty and mutual respect, and tolerance of those with different faiths and beliefs

- Ensure that personal beliefs are not expressed in ways that exploit pupils' vulnerability

SEN (D) – Special Educational Needs & Disabled
ADHD – Attention deficit hyperactivity disorder
Ritalin – Medication used to control ADHD
CLA/LAC – Child looked after/ Looked after child
FSM – Child receiving free school meals (their parent(s) or guardian(s) have to be receiving income support or more commonly known as 'benefits' to be eligible.
DIRT – Dedicated improvement and reflection time
WWW – What went well
EBI – Even better if
G&T – Gifted and talented
LA – Less able/lower ability
MA – Medium ability
HA – High ability
SLT – Senior management team
TLR bonus – teaching and learning responsibility bonus
PPA – Planning, Preparation and Assessment time

GCSE – General Certificate of Secondary Education
PGCE – Postgraduate Certificate of Education
TES – Times Education Standard

Ofsted/HMI – 'Her Majesty's' Education Inspectors. A waste of taxpayer's money and human resources, hugely overpaid, judge an entire teaching career and school based on statistics and a small selection of 20 minute lessons, and largely to blame for the current teaching crisis in the UK. Often old, out of touch, judge a subject which they have little or no understanding of, and love nothing more than to show off the power that they have been unjustifiably given. They make Dolores Umbridge from Harry Potter look like a harmless jelly bean. Their existence is continually enabled by brown nosing members of senior management in schools who want nothing more than to 'climb the ladder'.

Ofsted grading

1 – Outstanding

2 – Good

3 – Requires improvement

4 – Unsatisfactory/Just close it down immediately